HIS
OF THE
NATION
OF
ISLAM

Interview by
Elijah Muhammad
(Messenger of Allah)

Published by
Secretarius MEMPS Ministries

i

History
Of
The Nation of Islam

Copyright © 1993

Published by
Secretarius MEMPS Ministries
5025 North Central Avenue #415
Phoenix, Arizona 85012
Phone & Fax 602 466-7347
Email: cs@memps.com
Web: http://www.memps.com

ISBN10# 1-884855-88-1
EAN13# 978-1-884855-88-7

HISTORY OF THE NATION OF ISLAM

TABLE OF CONTENT

ACKNOWLEDGEMENT

We seek the assistance of Allah (God), Who came in the person of Master Fard Muhammad, through His Last and Greatest Messenger, the Most Honorable Elijah Muhammad.

We can never thank them enough for the Supreme Wisdom showered upon us; for the Messenger himself said, "He (Allah) gave it to me like a flowing spring or flowing fountain. The fountain has enough drink in it to give everyone drink who comes to drink. YOU DON'T NEED A NEW FOUNTAIN, JUST TRY DRINKING UP WHAT THIS FOUNTAIN HAS." Therefore, we avail ourselves of that water without hesitation, because we never get full. This means that the need for another fountain is totally obsolete.

I thank the MEMPS staff for their hard work in developing this great title, and pray that Allah (God) continue blessing us with His favor.

As-Salaam-Alaikum

Nasir Makr Hakim,
Minister of Elijah Muhammad, Messenger of Allah

vi

PREFACE

It is such an honor and noble privilege to be afforded the opportunity to not only come into the possession of the great lectures, writings and private utterances of the Honorable Elijah Muhammad, Last and Greatest Messenger of Allah, but as well, to make them available to those of our people who are thirsting for his pure word.

When reading what the Messenger states in this writing, one is actually given excellent answers to question every believer as well as non-believer have had, but didn't know how to ask. And who is better qualified to answer questions about the Messenger, the Nation of Islam and its history, than the Honorable Elijah Muhammad himself.

The Messenger eloquently and masterfully addresses subjects, which range from the first meeting of Allah (God), Who came in the Person of Master Fard Muhammad, himself; Master Fard Muhammad's origin, the race question, the Secrets of Gods, Are the Jews considered white, are the Turks Muslims, The New Book, just to name a few.

Much of this information has not previously been available; however, in light of the great necessity and our devotion to this much needed task, we pray to Allah (God), Master Fard Muhammad, that His Words, which were echoed, carried and personified by His Last and Greatest Messenger, the Honorable Elijah Muhammad, serve as a light in this time of great spiritual darkness and uncertainty.

In these troubled times of the Messenger's absence, the process of national self realization is taking it course. Those who were actually in the presence of the Messenger directly, those there by proxy and those now here are wrestling with our budding identity.

With history as a guide, it teaches us that as great splits and disagreements developed in years past after the departure of Messengers; whereas, those belonging to the physical bloodline thought they had more rights to the Messenger's legacy than those more consistent to the principles that he taught.

There is civil war between Orthodox Muslims and the enemy of them both is the cause, instigators, and yes, the mediators, although they are the ones who put one against the other, then mediates between them while ruling them both.

We were asked by the Messenger of Allah, Elijah Muhammad, "Can you fool a Muslim?" We answered, "Not nowadays." This is only possible if you have up to date truth to aid in identifying the time you're in and the necessary actions that goes with that time.

What they are fighting over is a "burnt offering." It had its value yesterday as a sign, but now that the fulfillment is present, it doesn't have the same value as it once had. This books points the way to the wide awake Muslim.

History of The Nation of Islam

We have been invited into the home of The Honorable Elijah Muhammad, leader of the Nation of Islam, better known to most people as the Black Muslims. Mr. Muhammad, it is great that you can sit down and chat with us for awhile, and explain some of his studies and some of his philosophy [and views] on religion.

THE FIRST MEETING BETWEEN THE SAVIOUR: MASTER FARD MUHAMMAD & HIS MESSENGER, ELIJAH MUHAMMAD

Question: Mr. Muhammad, what is the purpose, what is the goal of the Nation of Islam.

Messenger: It is to reform our people in America and put them to themselves in some place where they can go for themselves and do for themselves. I don't know of any other way that I could say it, other than to separate them and put them back to doing for themselves and furthering themselves.

Question: What is the background of the Nation of Islam in America?

1

Messenger: When I first heard of Islam it was in Detroit Michigan, back in the early fall of 1931, and I heard that there was a man teaching Islam by the name of Mr. Wallace Fard. At that time He used the initials W.D. Fard, that was in Detroit Michigan. When I heard what was said, I wanted to meet Him and I finally did. When I met Him, I looked at Him and it just came to me, that this is the Son of Man that the Bible prophesied would come in the last days of the world, and I couldn't get that out of me. I shook hands with Him and I said to Him, 'You are the One that the Bible prophesied would come at the end of the world under the name Son of Man and under the name The Second Coming of Jesus.'

And so, He looked at me a little stern, and then He smiled, put His head down beside my head then whispered in my ear and said these words, "Yes I am the One, but who knows that but yourself," and to "be quiet." He patted His hand on my shoulder, gave me kind of a little shove away around him. There was more present and He started talking to some of them.

About a month later, He told my wife to tell me to go ahead and start teaching out there in Hamtramck Michigan, that's in Detroit, I was living in Hamtramck at that time. So, He says to my wife, you tell him that he can go ahead, because I had wrote Him, and He received my letter and I was telling Him what I could not tell Him in the public. He said to me, "You go ahead and start teaching, and I will back you up." I started teaching that He was the answer to the prophesy of the coming of Jesus two thousand years after Jesus's birth, and

2

that this is the Man, at that time.

And so, I did begin teaching, that the Son of Man, or the second coming of Jesus is present. This is Him now, here among us. He didn't allow me to go too far with that kind of teaching while He was present; He told me, "You can do that after I am gone; don't talk to much about Me." He said, "Give them a little milk." That's the way He talked all the time. He hardly never would say anything direct. He would give it to you in a way that you would have to learn just exactly what He meant by what He said. And so, He said, "You cannot give babies meat." I understood what He was referring to. And so He said, "Give the little baby milk." He said, "When I am gone, then you can say whatever you want to about Me." I was not too much learned into scripture at that time, and I had not studied too much, but from a child's age up, wanted to learn the scripture, because my father was a preacher, and I always, since a child, wanted to help him or take his place one day as a preacher.

I was always studying the Bible and had read much about the coming of the judgement, the coming of God, Jesus returning to resurrect the dead and all like that. I had studied much of that. And so, all of His conversations and teachings corresponded with what I had learned of the scripture; therefore, I had become a hundred percent convert. On His leave of us, He began to tell me what I may expect, what will come to pass, and what I should do to reform my people and make them acceptable to the Islamic people. I also must teach them that they must change completely in the way of

3

righteousness and that they would have to forego the name that they was in, and that He would give them all a name Himself and said to me that He must.

He used to teach me night and day. We used to sit sometime from the early part of the night until sunrise and after sunrise. All night long for about two years or more. He was with us three years or a little better, and I was constantly around Him and He was constantly teaching me teaching things of Islam: what is to come and what was before. This is the way that we began. He first gave me a name at that time; that name was Karriem. He called me Elijah Karriem. Later, about a year before He left us, He give me the name Muhammad. He changed the name. He said, "I will give you a better name than Karriem; you take Muhammad, My name." And so, that was about it. He as well named all of my family Muhammad.

THE HISTORY OF THE SAVIOUR: HIS ORIGIN, "DISAPPEARANCE," AND WHEREABOUTS

Question: Where did Fard Muhammad come from, and why did He disappear and where did He go? Where is He now?

Messenger: He taught us that He was born in Mecca, Arabia, and that He had come in and out of this country for about twenty (20) years before ever making himself known to us. He had enrolled in California University and He lived with a white family out there while He was going to the University. How long He went to this University, I don't know, but He said that He did go to this University and enrolled there and other Universities He mentioned to me, and finally He told me this, that He had studied every educational system of the civilized world, and that He could speak 16 languages fluently and write ten of them. He said that He had been studying for us. What He meant to teach us and to reform us for forty two years, He said to me. His Father, He said - I should let the world know these things which He said to me, as I never have went too much into His birth and into His sayings of what took place; so, I am going to tell this. I intend to give a full description of it on the twenty sixth (26th) of next month in

Chicago, and give it in detail, but at this time, I can say this:

His Father wanted a son that would go and search for the lost people of mine. He said they had it in the Qur'an, they had it in the Bible or scriptures that there would be a lost member at the time of the resurrection and that they had to find That one because it did not give the location. He said that His Father wanted to make a son that would be able to go and search all the civilizations of the Earth to locate this people and when He found them, teach them and make a disciple of His Own of them to teach them and try and get them together and return them again to there own people. And so, he said He was that Man.

His Father's first child was a girl. He smiled and said, "He had to make another try for Me." And His Mother, He said, was a white woman. He said, "My father went up in the mountains to choose My Mother in order to get a child that looked like the people that had this particular member among them so that He could get among them more successfully, and that He was the One. His Mother, He said, was a white woman, and His Father was a Blackman. Yes sir, He said that His Father was darker than us, we whom the Saviour was talking to at the time; His Father is a real dark man. He was still alive, and He said this is the way that this took place. He said, "I'm here, and I want you to know I love you, and My Father made Me for you, and We want you to know yourself and put you on to your own kind."

He taught us about our being away from our people and that we were unqualified to mix with them, because they were Islamic people and we were not, and that we didn't even know who we were. And so, that was true and that was easy to get over to us.

I've taken all of this and talked to my people and have been teaching them the same, but I never went into His Birth, how His Father trained Him and what all He said about that, because I feared my people would not believe since they believed mostly in spirits: That God is a spirit or something like that and He's not flesh and blood, He's not visible, and because of this, I am very slow about getting it over to my people, but now they will just have to take it or leave it. These are facts and this is according to the Bible that the Son of Man would come and not the son of a spirit. This I want to make clear to them and those who believe in the spirit being God and not Man. The main base of it all is to show forth who's God, for He's not who they thought He was; He's in man and man is God. So, that's the way that goes, and in Chicago on the twenty sixth (26th) of next month, I will go into detail about His birth, childhood, manhood and so forth, and into scripture that is relating this coming of God in Man.

The Son, the scholars know, it only means the way He has given it to me. He was born of His Father to go after the Lost-Found Sheep. The Bible calls it, and the Jesus made it into beautiful parables that He will search for the Lost Sheep and all like that. All of this has now been fulfilled and this is it that we are now living in. My work from Him was to teach my people these facts, and to reform them and make them what they should be: as they are children, the Bible teaches, from God, but they are lost in evil and practice evil. They must now forego evil and except righteousness, because they are creatures of righteousness.

Question: What happened to Fard Muhammad, and why did He disappear?

Messenger: Well, that happened like this: After He had given to me what He wanted to give to me, which was the teachings and the work of preparedness for our people, it was not necessary for Him to remain here among us; so, He had taken His leave, as it is said in the Qur'an: that the people are not worthy that God remain among them; however, He makes a Messenger of that people, that through that Messenger, He will reach the people - through Him, and the Bible verifies the same. And so, He left and He gave me a hint about His return, but there is just as much prophesy that He will not return as there is of His returning, because the Bible says He will send His angels and they will take care of the gathering of His people. I don't expect Him to return in person, not like that, because there is to much for us to look forward to that He will not. It is not really necessary if He is going to send His Own people, as they're referred to as angels, to gather the believers of my people, it's not necessary.

Question: Where did He go and where is He now?

8

Messenger: Well, that is something that we actually cannot say. If one would open up such truth, such as the truth of God to the people. I do think that He's within His rights to stay out of the sight of the people until He has won everything to Himself; as the Bible refers to it like this: He's something like a king looking for a kingdom. And that He goes and visits the people, then He leaves the people, goes away and wait until the time when He can secure the kingdom. Then He returns to the people that He had made Himself manifest to. So I think that's a pretty good answer.

THE BEGINNING OF RACES

According to what Master Fard Muhammad taught me on the origin of the races, they number around four, and from these four races of people, they have produced many different types of people, but they are not independent in their beginning, they came from one. We have lots of various colored people all over the Earth from brown to white, we're not all the same color. As a result of intermixing with such colors as black, brown, yellow, and red and white, this has produced many other various colors. The origin of it, according to the teachings of Master Fard Muhammad to me, was from a Scientist or God - we see him as a God. Back six thousand years ago, a master grafting work on the human being started to produce a new civilization, or a new race of people from the original race of people or aboriginal people.

This man, Yakub, discovered in the germ of the black man, that he had two people in him, and had learned through study and experimenting on the germ that this second germ could produce a powerful people that would be able to rule that which they came from. They would be able to rule for around six thousand years or until the father or the aboriginal people produce One superior to his man. He had taken, through experimental work on the germ of man, a people of what we call today a white race, but before he produced that white race, he produced a brown race, then he produced a yellow race and so on. There lies his first grafting of the black man according to the teachings of Master Fard Muhammad, Whom we see and know today as being God in person.

From the grafting in it's first stage, he (Yakub) had a brown race of people from a black people, and it taken him, according to the teachings of God, two hundred years to produce that brown race, and he kept up the process of killing off the brown or the darker one and marrying the lighter one with the lighter one, and in another two hundred years, he had a yellow race of people. In this length of time, these brown people were spreading and migrating over the earth to find them a home to themselves.

And so, when the yellow race was produced, they too started migrating over the Earth, and from the yellow race, about two hundred years, this grafting kept in process. They were on the same island according to the teachings of Almighty God that were taught to me, by Allah (God), Who came in the Person of Master Fard Muhammad, to Whom Praises is due forever.

10

During that two hundred years of keeping up birth control laws, this is what he established. He established it on this island in his lab where he was working, we call it a human lab to produce his man. And from this yellow race he had a white race two hundred years later from them. And this was the end of his work. This was the man he was trying to get to: a white race.

That concluded the total time of his grafting the white out of black in six hundred years, and this figure tallies with the Bible's teaching of the man being created in six days. The days here mean a hundred years each, six hundred years. And this also tallies with the creation of the universe: six. The whole entire universe, according to the Qur'an was also created in six periods of time. And so Mr. Yakub, the Mighty Scientist of that time, produced his man on six because it tallied with the creation of the universe and it was according to this number that he could do his work: They would be masters, gods to rule the Earth, the people and everything of life, for six thousand years. At the end of six thousand years, the aboriginal people will have produced another One mightier than Yakub in wisdom and knowledge and He would be equal with that One that created the heavens and the Earth. And He would have the power and the infinite wisdom to make His Word Be as the first One. This is the Man we have before us today, to Whom praise is due.

Master Fard Muhammad is that Man Who has the wisdom or the knowledge of how the creation took place in the first place. What I mean: The creation of the universe, how it

11

took place and how life and everything began down to six thousand years of Mr. Yakub and his world, and the knowledge of the world to come of which He Himself is the God of. He's the God of the next world, He's planning it now. And that world that He will set up, we see now gradually merging in, will be forever. There will be no change in that one, because the scientists just don't see through the future of any other change. They don't have to much knowledge of His change, as He has not let go yet. He brought me up pretty close, but He has not as yet opened up. We have it in the Bible and Qur'an, that eyes have not seen nor ears have heard, and it has not entered into the heart of us what He will do, but we get little inklings. Now we are right in His time, and we do know that He is going to bring about a complete change.

As I've studied for thirty three years after His coming, I have learned my own self from study of His words, what He said to me. It won't be a world like we see today, nothing of the kind, not even to the Orthodox Muslims. Their world will not even be considered in His world. The Master Scientist or God, six thousand years ago, Mr. Yakub, did not make his world like our world, on the basis of our world. We have a completely new world and a new people in you. So will the great Mahdi, Master Fard Muhammad, He will also build a new world and a new people.

He did tell me how we would start taking a change in a new people. Now just exactly what we will look like, I'm not to sure of that, but I believe He's going right back to the origin; He's going to make a better people. What I mean to say is a people that will be more stronger physically and they will be taught in such way that they can live much longer. Individuals will live probably a thousand or more years.

In teaching something about the history, not the history, but about the people on Mars, He often would refer to me that just think of them living twelve hundred of our Earth years, He said, and we dying in less than a hundred years. It gives me an idea that He wants to make a people that will live a thousand or more years. This is also hinted at in the Bible and Qur'an, this teaching, and so now He intends to do just that.

According to the way that Almighty God taught me, in the Person of Master Fard Muhammad, that in grafting anything, even fruit, or the life of animals like the birds, or fowl, all of these things can be grafted to make another self out of them. So you have gotten just this: You have made many things from the aboriginal. And today we see much of your world that you have produced through grafting. And you're a master at that, I must say, you're a master at grafting because the father, Mr. Yakub, was a master.

Question: One thing I noted here in our conversation, when you say "you,..."

Messenger: When I say you, I don't mean you personally, I mean the white race, and the black race is what we are here discussing. According to what I have been taught of God, as you know, that I don't know anything and I didn't know anything before this Master Mind came to me or the Wise

Man Who I teaches to be God in Person, and I believe I'm right according to the scripture, and I know I'm right according to what He has said, and how it corresponds with the prophetic sayings of the prophets concerning him, or one coming in this time. In grafting, lets get back to there, to answer that question. In grafting a life from a life that is original, that which we graft from the original, regardless to what life it is, it is weaker than that which it was grafted from. We are reducing the power of that original when we graft from it. When we graft fruit, the fruit that we graft is not the equal to that which we graft it out of. And so it is when it comes to life, whether it's birds, whether it's a beast, animals, or what not.

In cats, such as the cat family, all the grafted of it's family is lesser in power than the original lion, and that which is grafted from the original lion is not to be trusted to much as with leopards and in the other cats from the lion family. These cats from the lion family are more dangerous and cannot be trusted like we can this original lion. The original lion, we can take him, make him lie around us even at an old age, and we can still trust him, but we can't trust this leopard and these other cats, because they have, by nature, something evilly wicked that came through the grafting. He comes upon us while we're not looking at him;before we know it, he's destroyed us. So we don't trust him, but we will trust the original lion. Get them when he's a little cub, and we can bring him up like he's any other house cat, walk around and play with him till he's an old man. So it is with the human being.

THE SECRET OF GOD: YAKUB

According the words to us from Almighty God Allah, in the Person of Master Fard Muhammad, to Whom Praise is due forever, Who has now made manifest the secret of the Gods. This is the secret of the Gods that we are discussing, and not that of mere human beings. In taking a god from a God, the god that came from the original God or race of people or nation or aboriginal, is easy to make into what the name means, devil, because by grafting the very nature, the entire human being, is more fit for the teaching of grafting or law, than something other than that which he came from.

Now as we see in fruit, fowl and in the grafting of animals and what not, that the product always become lesser and lesser as we continue to graft. Now we come to the white man and the black man: Here we have a black man, original, we can't locate his birth, he's the aboriginal human being of the Earth. Now from him he has produced brown, yellow, red, and white, through the master wisdom of grafting of the God, Yakub. And in this work of Mr. Yakub, taking the white man out into, what we would say today, the fifth stage of the family, he became the fifth man, and the most distinct of all. He's a new man to every one of us, new race of people. And with a nature and wisdom that is absolutely new, contrary to the aboriginal, the black man. Before Mr. Yakub, they had not never reached this particular point of unalike attract or like repel, but in his producing a people, this is the base on which he set. This was his work which produced an unlike people,

15

and an unalike people would be able to attract the like. In this way, he had perfected an idea of how to rule a like. Unalike attract and like repel; therefore, being able to produce this unalike, it will attract a like and will be able to rule a like until a like produces something to prevent a like from being attracted by unalike.

This refers to the Gods. We are tinkering, or rather, we're into what the scientist say, into the wisdom of God, and how Their ideas worked, and how Their ideas come to perfection.

Here we have a man produced from the Original man, and that man we call the white man. The white man, we say, is the devil. Why, because of his physical weakness, caused by coming into being from original man, or aboriginal people of the Earth. With the wise master mind of his father, the God that made him, he is able, with that weak physical form taken from the original form or original man, to rule the strong man, which is mentioned so much by the scholars, among the scholars and scientist that write history and discuss this same point in their language that which the masses cannot understand.

This made it easy to teach the man a wisdom contrary and opposed to the wisdom of right, because Yakub was not after producing a man that was of the same or would think the same, like the one he was taken him from. He had to make his world so attractive, that he would attract the minds of the world that he came out of until that world produced a man that would overcome him in wisdom - ours is superior in

16

wisdom - and would make His people equally superior by teaching them the origin of everything that took place and then the white race would have no more attraction upon the people that they came from.

After they learned the origin of their creation and how it came about and how their God gave them the wisdom of the know-how to rule that which they came out of; we could say, in words, the original overtakes himself again. Now he starts all over again to manufacture or to produce another man as we have this in history and prophesy, that the God at the end of the world of the white man will produce a new heaven or new civilization, we say heaven or kingdom on Earth, but it only means people, a new people and they have a new kind of a wisdom that is superior to the present.

BY ONE MAN SIN ENTERED

Question: We still don't know how the evil got in there.

Messenger: Yes, after Mr. Yakub making the man, white from black, then the question is how yet did he become evil? This was done through the grafting too. He taught all of the nurses and doctors; whereas, the doctors and the nurse were the main ones He used. In the grafting of the child or the white out of black, he taught the nurses that as soon as the baby comes to birth, if it's a black baby, then give it over the cremators or to some wild beast: destroy that child. If the mother is not looking at the child or watching you too closely, nurse, take a needle, a sharp needle, and prick it in the brain of the baby and tell the mother that her child was still-born; we call them dead under that name still-born. This process went on throughout the brown child for another browner one. If that lesser brown was killed, and the browner was saved, the lighter one, or we say, the lighter was saved all throughout. By having this murder inserted into the mind of the nurses to destroy the darker or the browner or the yellow, until they got to the white one, once the white one came in, naturally this was in the nature of the white one: to then object to anything other than white as a human being; consequently, he would try to destroy or kill anything that is coming into his race.

Question: We finished the nurses killing the children.....
Messenger: Now about these nurses' position and teaching: It was to murder everything of darker color or any color that was pertaining to the darker color up to the white baby and that was the end of the grafting, and this murderer, as Jesus mentioned it himself in the Bible there in John 8:44. He mentioned it as the making of one, coming from the father of a liar and murderer. The lie was inserted also into this grafting. This teaching, or rather sayings, of the nurse that Yakub had given to the nurse to tell the mother, when the black baby is born: that you have given birth to an angel baby and let us take this angel baby to heaven. This angel baby will get a room in heaven or apartment for you, and when you die you will go right to your baby. It was a very clever trick that was easily accepted by the mother, and the mother would let the

18

nurse take the baby away from them; to heaven she thought they were taken him, but it was to be murdered. Yakub had told the nurse that when you take the baby away from the mother, give this black baby over to a beast and let the beast eat it up, or give it to a cremator and let the cremator burn the baby. This was carried out by Yakub's workers and he forced this law to be obeyed by killing some of the workers just to put fear in the others, to make them do it. Not that these workers was guilty of anything like breaking the law, but he did that to force other workers to do what he said, put fear in them, and make them obey the law. And the law was carried out to the letter and spirit. And so, the people nursed this until this law of killing the baby and telling these lies to the mother of your baby, black babay, being an angel baby and it will go to heaven and secure you a room, and when you die you will come right up and join your baby.

When the browner baby came, the nurses were ordered by Yakub to tell that mother, you have given birth to a holy baby and this baby, we want you to take care of and for the next six weeks the nurse will be helping you, I think it was six weeks or six months, I think six weeks, yes. The mother will be helped by the nurse to wrap her baby, put it on the right road and she will help you. This brown baby was carefully watched and as soon as it gets old enough to marry, marry those to another brown one, and then they would produce a child a little browner than they, and this process kept on until they had driven out the very last stage of the black, brown, yellow, and produced a white baby. That was the end of the grafting, and in this white baby, he had murderer of the darker one put in him from the very beginning. This is what the Jesus was referring to, when saying that he was a murderer from the beginning, because the process of getting him was on the basis of murdering the black one and saving the lighter one. The lie that he was produced in, was the lie that the nurse told the mother of the child, and this comes down through the mother to the child, which makes the child be very tricky and saying things that were not true.

Question: What is your view of the character of the white man?

Messenger: The characteristics of the white man is evil. He was made like that through nature. Naturally he was made like that through the grafting.

THE DEVIL OR SATAN: IS THERE A DIFFERENCE?

Question: And as you said previously, the white man is the devil, or satan or both are they the same?

Messenger: No sir. Satan has a wider spread, we would say, than the devil. We can see a devil cat out there, a devil animal, or a devil; we could call most any grafted thing a devil, you see, but actually when we say satan, we mean a man or a people whose wickedness is not confined to themselves, it spreads, and others are affected by their wickedness.

Now we can take this question up from just what we said here in the grafting and through the grafting of this people. They were being separated all the while, the brown was separated from the yellow, and yellow separated from the white. So, separation was the answer to the whole process of the creation, and the whole universe; everything is separated. There's nothing put in the sphere of another one. Everything is independent within it's own sphere. So, since the white man brought us out of our original land and people and has kept us here without taking us back or without the knowledge of how to get back for the past four hundred years, this knowledge God has been brought to us, and the answer is now only separation. We must go back to our own. You came here from Europe. You probably will have to return to your home in order to fulfill that which is written of the scripture by the prophets who put it in there. I think I read this somewhere in the Bible where it says at that time every man will go to his own people and country, meaning at the end of the rule of the white people, who will then separate themselves and every man will go like they did in the beginning. At the beginning they were separated, the black went to itself, the brown went to itself, yellow went to itself, white went to itself.

THE NEGRO PROBLEM: SEPARATION IS THE KEY

Question: Do I understand, you feel that, the only ones who would be left here would be the American Indian, is that correct?

Messenger: Well if the Bible and Qur'an is to be fulfilled and they will, the Qur'an even mentions too, of the great separation. And that original owner should take his place. Wherever his sphere is at, he should go there. If the Indian was here as God has taught me sixteen thousand years (16,000) which would put him ten thousand years on the planet ahead of you, he's ahead of the white race. Now, if he is going to carry out what we read, then in the future, the Indians will posses that country again.

Question: What country would the black man go to?

Messenger: Well, the black man, he has a great vast country to go to: anywhere. Not to say that he's confined to Africa, he's not confined to Africa, he could live here, he could live there, because the whole thing is his home, the whole Earth is the Blackman's home. This is mentioned also in the Bible, as Jesus prophesied of it so many times, he says, "The Earth belongs to the Lord." It's referring to the aboriginal people here. A lord, we say in English, means a master or masters. Originally the Earth belonged to the black man and these other

22

colors came out of him; therefore, he has number one, first a possession of where ever he would like to live. If the black man, here, would return to Africa, he still one day would spread over the Earth, as he's in Australia, he's in the Islands of the Pacific, he's everywhere anyway. Hardly no place, now in Europe where he has not actually been in power there for a long, long, time, that part of our planet was not inhabited by a black man for a long old time.

Question: Tell me about your plans or plan here.

Messenger: Now this is what we have on the back or last page of our paper, Muhammad Speaks. That program concerning land and a place for the so-called American Negro, could be made by the government to bring about a cessation or stop of these clashes that's now going on, which will finally produce a war that will destroy one or the other of us here in America. We must now consider the presence of the God in this particular problem of the so-called American Negro and his once slave-master. He also is intervening in it and we just cannot say that we're going to forget about His ideas that he give to us through the mouth of the prophets of old, concerning this time. We have to consider them, and we have to bow finally to His desire. His desire today is to separate we, the once slaves of the white race here, and give us a chance to go for self, freedom for self. Our time, according to the prophesy given to Abraham, is up; wherein, it stated that his people would go into a strange land, and while there, serve strangers for the duration of four hundred years; this is up now. This prophesy did not refer to the Jews at all, this refers

23

to us. At that time, God would judge the people and so on and so on. So, as I see it, there is much misunderstanding among the average white people concerning this prophesy; that we have reached an end of it and now to continue trying to force the once-slave into living in a subjected state with them, being subject to them all the while and not even given much a chance to go for themselves; yet, they don't want to give them justice, because if the white man would give us justice, that would also help us to go for self.

Being deprived of justice prevents us from even going for self. Being at peace with the white man and ourselves, it's a growing thing of unrest among the Negro. Hatred is growing towards his white master, because now he's seeing the evil of his white master against him, that at any price, he don't want to give him justice. In his courts daily he's deprived of justice, and he's sent off to prison sometimes just for nothing, just because he is a Negro, and that there is no one to force the white man to give him justice in court. This, the Negro is looking at day and night now, then out in the streets he's being beaten up by the police force, because he's people that is deprived of justice and the police know that. He can beat him and kill him; there's no such thing as the government bringing him before the court and condemning him of the death of a Negro or to send him to prison for an unnecessarily short duration. This is now in the eyes and hearts of the Negro and the masses of the Negroes. The masses of them are growing and growing under the same idea or in the same idea. There's no justice for us by these people. Why should we continue to try to force ourselves to live with them? They don't like even

24

our very looks. They hate us, and before their supreme courts, if we take our case before them, meaning the nine judges, there is no justice coming from them for us; they're just the same as this one here in the city. So here, hopelessness put in the heart of the Negro today; he's hopeless, and he don't have no more faith in his white master to give him nothing but hell, to tell you the truth - using the common language of being mistreated. He just don't see nothing but that.

We have a little small organization that we called the NAACP, headed towards trying to get the right to vote, thinking that that right will bring more justice for his people, but we don't see that being no solution for the problem. The problem won't be solved there, because he's going to vote for white people to rule him right on, and why should he vote for the white man to go into office, then after getting into office as President or Congressman, he still suffers. That don't lighten his burden under the merciless hand or the merciless heart of the judge sitting in court. And that is what is going on.
The best thing, if the white man of America would like to lighten this burden, which he's creating on himself, he could easily take the large country in which we have helped him to produce, maintain, and have fought for his independence, [is to give us part]. No more do we have the idea that we were fighting for ourselves, because we know now that we can live out of America. We don't have to live in America; we can get out of America, and live elsewhere. By the Negro becoming a Muslim makes it very easy, because the Islamic world is a world that will live forever.

There's no such thing of an opponent of Islam thinking that they can destroy Islam, it's impossible, that's the impossible. And so, by we accepting Islam, as the Bible teaches, it's like accepting life, and it is accepting life. We will live and rule forever under righteousness which is only Islam, which means entire submission to the will of God. We will rule under that forever, but to say that some forces can destroy us, we can't be destroyed, because the God of the righteous is to wise. His Word is Be. Whenever He get ready to do a thing.... He's capable of making a man, turning a man's science around, backwards in him. You just can't do anything about that. If the God is powerful enough to turn our science around in our brains, and make us to think less, as the backward word means here, it means to go back over something that is not equal or not have the power to progress in our thinking.

The problem of separating is easy. We have once been separated and it's easy to separate, and is a easy thing for the USA to do. She has plenty of territory. She could easily put us aside in some part and, well we don't want to give up no property. You are paying for us to live where you are, wherever we are, we don't own it, you're paying for it. Therefore, it's easy for you to just clear off a place over here. It could be said, well, you take that place and I'll take this one over here, and we will live here, and you live there. I will help you to get started and it won't be permanent, you must learn someday to go for yourself. I'll set a time about a quarter of a century, about twenty, twenty five years. I think we will be able to produce the necessities of life for ourself. We can get along in peace to ourselves, because we're going to be dominated by Islam. We're not going to have no rulers other than Islam over us, because the average so-called Negro who have not the knowledge of Islam, cannot rule himself in peace; he will destroy himself if put alone like he is; he will eat himself up. But we will put a stop to that; in fact, we won't even start with it. We will have a national brotherhood among ourself under Islam and there will be no ruler, but a man of Islam.

100% HATRED BETWEEN THE RACES

Question: Mr Muhammad, in 1961, Esquire Magazine [quoted you as saying that there is] 100% hatred between the races.

Messenger: A hundred percent hatred between the two races. When we refer to it spiritually, it is. There is a hundred percent hatred between a black and a white man here in America spiritually, and something must be done whenever the spiritual side of people become that near, or to that point. Something is going to be done, because they will produce something to take it away. We're just at the cross-roads of separation and therefore, we just have to go ahead, one his way, and the other his way, because there's no way to get along in peace. We can't reverse it, we've continued toward ourself in the way of dislike for each other to be subject to the other. This is the main thing. Not that we hate one another's color, the color could be peaceful to us, we have all kinds of colors in the universe to look at, but it is the nature or characteristic of us that we hate, that's the thing.

MALCOLM'S "DEFECTION"

Question: What was the reason for the defect of Malcolm X and what is he doing now?

Messenger: Well, I would look at Malcolm's act of hypocrisy, defection as you say, as the Qur'an and Bible speaks of such people. He had followed me for a few years. All that he knew and how to apply it came from me. Now, to become an evil person to me..., he had it on him, in these few years. Therefore he felt that he was now a big man before the public, and this seemed to have been his desire. He wanted to be seen and heard or he wanted to exalt himself above his teacher; therefore, after I reminded him back in December, a year ago when the assassination of the president took place, I warned him for not having any respect for the Chief of the land in whom everyone had voted mostly, probably, but he and just a few of us, that you must show respect for those in authority regardless to their belief, whether it is against Islam or for Islam, and that we are to respect them and that the President of the country is our President too. We live under him as well as the Christian, because we don't have no President for

28

ourself here. We must respect the President of the land regardless to what religion he is. This act that he made was not in accord with our teachings, so I dispensed with Malcolm for awhile. That was my mind at that time: to just sit him down from the public for awhile. If he would react favorably and promise me he would not make such mistake again in the future. But he began to get restless, seemingly, and impatient to sit and wait until I tell him to come back on the platform again. And so he seemed to have created an evil spirit within himself; therefore, he gave up following me and said that he would go for himself as the paper stated at that time, and we still have the clippings of the paper wherein he said that he would give it up and that he would set up Mosque Incorporated under his own guidance and that he would go for himself. I know I couldn't go for myself, because I was not able to go for myself before the coming of Allah, and I'm certainly not able to continue going for myself now after He put me on the right path. I still cannot stay in it without His guidance.

I felt very strange about the young man saying that he was going for himself. I know that meant complete failure because he could not be successful in trying to build up a thing, like a religious teaching of Islam here under my mission or beside my mission or above it or whatever he was trying to do, because my work is divine work. Allah has chosen me for the work, and therefore, the God just don't change like that and put down one and take up another one. If one baby don't act right, He will spank him anyway and make him act right, but he don't mean to kill the baby and put another baby in his place. So Malcolm didn't have this kind of knowledge, or he would not have acted as he has acted. I think justice is after Malcolm and that pretty soon he will be on his knees trying to crawl back to just that which he left.

Question: Do you think there are any alternatives for him?

Messenger: There are no alternatives for him.

Question: Do you know what he's doing currently, what his current activities are?

Messenger: I don't know what Malcolm is doing now, and I don't keep any record of any hypocrite that becomes a hypocrite. Any person that becomes a hypocrite, I don't keep no watch over them. They do whatever they want to, because I know ultimately they will be back again anyway.

Question: Has his current activities had any effect on the Nation of Islam in America, on your followers? Did he take other people with him?

Messenger: We can't tell whether Malcolm has taken any people of sizeable number from us. We continue to increase in number daily and we never miss them. All the older ones that was here with us when he left us, we have with us right on, except just a few. Not enough for us to tell in the checking of the records. We still have more with us today than we had a year or so ago when Malcolm left. We have more; we are greater in number and all of most of the older one is still with

30

us and even those that went out with him. Part of them have now returned and the other part is still begging to return. Even my own son is begging me now in a way to try to get back, my son Wallace in Chicago.

Question: Your grandson as well?

Messenger: I don't have any letter from my grandson, but I have a letter from my own son, he wrote that he would like to return.

ON VIOLENCE

Question: You felt that God Himself would not be with the Muslims if they became, if they were violent, the fact that violence is not a part of Muslim.... can you just restate that for me, say it again of how the fact that violence is not a part of....

Messenger: No, when it comes to violence or fighting, that's not inherent in us because the righteous could not be classified, or they could not be righteous if such characteristics was in them or they practice such. They couldn't be called righteous people. The Muslim is not, according to his own scripture, never to result to violence and he's taught to only, we say, use self defense if attacked, but never to be the attacker; in fact, it's against divine law, and God Himself, is not on the side of the Muslim if he resorts to such things as violence. And he could easily be classified as non-Muslim.

31

THE PURPOSE OF THE FRUIT OF ISLAM (F.O.I.)

Question: Is the purpose of the F.O.I. simply protection or self defense?

Messenger: We don't say self defense or so much as discipline, this is a practice mostly of health than anything else. Being active you know, physically, this comes under the headings mostly of health exercise. As they don't mix to much with the Christians in taking exercises less sometimes they get in such centers, causes friction, and I warned them to stay out of any place where ever it might produce friction between the Christian and the Muslim. So, they takes exercise, they practice this and it also serves and act as self defense for the body. Like you, in high school and college, practice to defend yourself in case of attack. But not on the scale as a national base for fighting some aggressive people or nation, because we would need atomic bombs and hydrogen bombs. We're practicing nothing like that, but hands will be no weapons in a war that we see today in this modern warfare.

This thing about fighting: My followers don't get that kind of teaching, only just for self defense. But arming themselves with cardinal weapons, no, I am forbidden by God to do so. Master Fard Muhammad, to Whom Praise is due forever, taught me not to allow my followers to carry so much as a pin knife to attack no one with. I think now it has been nationally and universally known that my followers doesn't resort to no such thing, and if anyone is found, I mean the followers of mine, carrying anything like weapons, we call them in and take them away from them, and put them out of the Mosque for so many months until we learn that he's not the man that carries weapons. <u>Now keep them in his home, he must not take them out of his home, so that we will not be charged with violence, or attacking no one with weapons.</u>

THE DESTRUCTION OF NORTH AMERICA

Question: Can you describe for us the destruction of North America as you foresee it?

Messenger: Now I come to the destruction of North America, the doom of North America. Allah gave it to me, but it only corresponded with that which is prophesied in the Bible and Qur'an, that America would be destroyed, It's not called America, but the wicked will be destroyed in the last day, and He said to me that it would be done, but now I don't know when exactly it's going to take place. It depends on the act of the people. We were talking about territory somewhere where my people and myself can live to ourselves to keep from running into conflicts with the white man. This depends on that kind of act of the white man. How he would treat the so-called American Negroes that goes over to Islam. <u>There never will become no such thing as a total destruction of American people</u>, the white, until they try to destroy us. When they make war on us or start trying to kill us, that belief, that will bring the war, as it is written. We don't make no such acts that will inflame them to attack us, but we believe they will attack us someday or another, just because of our righteousness, not no aggressive act that we will make against them. We have nothing to fight them with other than our hands; therefore, we are not so foolish to run into guns with our hands unless we are sure that God is with us. We don't care nothing about weapons when we know that God is with us, because they just don't avail against us, because they are used by man, and God have power over man, that meaning, He have power over his weapons. And so, we don't, and is not going to, do anything to anger him but righteousness. We feel that even righteousness will anger him to the extent that someday or another, he'll attack, and want to kill, and that will bring about the total destruction of America.

As long as the present so-called Negro want to go along and suffer whatever punishment that the white race put upon him, he agrees to be his follower, there will be no such thing as any punishment hardly coming to the whiteman against that servant of his. But now that servant of God, of Allah, that's where he gets in trouble.

Question: Why will just North America be destroyed?

34

HISTORY OF THE NATION OF ISLAM

Messenger: Because North America is the one who enslaved us, you see, America is the one who has helped us out of the circle of freedom, justice, and equality. Ever since America's white people brought us here under John Hawkins, the first slave trader that was successful in bringing a ship load of our people, or, bringing some slaves here, I don't know how many he brought, I don't know about that, there's various estimations or histories of it. According to the history, he was the first. Ever since then, we've been the same subject, and the worst part about it, the white man of America seems to hate his slave with a most vehement hatred. He deals with his slave as though he is his most hated enemy. He loves to look at him like an experiment, or mistreat him as though he captured him in war, or like he's is an enemy of war against him and was trying to destroy his country, or destroy his race. That's the way he's treated. He's not treated like a slave, just a common slave, because after a slave stays with his master for centuries, then the master should try to treat him right and protect him. But not like he's an enemy among him. We are treated like an enemy instead of a slave. We don't say that we don't eat the same food you eat, you give us the same food, we don't say that you don't give us the same clothes. In fact, we have access to even the luxury, the best of it, if we are able, if we are able to afford it. You don't deprive us from that, but the thing of it is only in some instances we are deprived of it in equal employment, and other ways like in high taxes. We pay them in equal with the white citizen of America. Most of the country, that's another injustice we suffer. We shouldn't be taxed, because we don't have anything to be taxed for, only that which you give us. You give us a job, that's okay to you, but we didn't produce the job, you produced it. As we the children from your once servitude slaves, so we still have nothing, only what you gave us. When you give us anything, you tax us so heavy, until you just takes right back what you give us. That's injustice. We should be actually exempt from taxes, because we have nothing, and have never been given equal chances to get something. In order to pay the slave for something good he has done, we should be exempt from taxes, because we go to your war. We have to fight to maintain your independence, in our continued suffering under free slavery or status that we are in. So, I don't think that this is also anything good on the white man's part and the world also knows this as well as I. I don't mean the world of white mankind, I mean the world of my people. Black, brown, yellow, and red people, they all know this, and they all grieves over this same thing when it's discussed among them: That we are deprived of every justice, not one justice, but every justice. We are not recognized as human beings, not to say civil rights as citizens here in America, but not even a human being. We have been made, or rather, the white man makes us to look like that even now to the outside world. And we are the product that he made himself and this way he makes mockery of his own work. He did not make us his equal.

Question: I would like to get a picture, because you know, this is the only really good interview I've ever seen. Would you have any objection Mr. Muhammad?

Messenger: Oh no sir. I don't have no objection.

Question: Eric Hoffer in the New York Times wrote quite a complimentary article in the New York Times, would you comment, he's a San Franciscan, and he is a Long Shoreman.

Messenger: Yes sir, when I first saw his name I was thinking him to be some scientist or scholar something like that in New York someplace, but when I learned he was a Long Shoreman...

Question: He was a very scholarly Long Shoreman.
Messenger: Yes sir he is a scholar alright.

IMMEDIATE PROBLEMS THAT CONFRONTS THE NATION OF ISLAM

Question: What do you feel are the most immediate and pressing problems confronting your movement?

Messenger: Well, the most pressing problem, number 1, it is to get the leadership of our people to see that they're going after it the wrong way, the wrong way of trying to get justice for the people. This is not the right way to get freedom, justice, and equality.

37

Question: In other words, their goals are incorrect?

Messenger: Incorrect is right, because they want to be accepted in the race of the whites as brothers or would desire to force the white race. To see that by nature they should be accepted as equally, you know, related, as brothers by the creation of God and all like that. This is their misunderstanding, and what we would like to make them to see is that you just can't become a member of that which God didn't make you a member of. It only ruins the races to mongrualize themselves. It just ruins and destroys a people, and it's also indecency to even think about these things like that. This is one thing that is a problem for us. We don't know whether sometimes to say they actually have overdue love for the white people, to want to become one of them, or that they're ignorant, or that they are fascinated by the wealth of the white people and thinking that they will share more into the wealth of the white people. Which again we try to teach them that you should not be carried away with the wealth of the white people then. Since your people and my people helped create and produce. Regardless to being denied it, they also can easily see that you was a piece of property of theirs, and they had a right to do whatever they wanted to with their own property. And so, this is hard, you know, this kind of solution to the problem is hard to get them to see as it is written, the dead is hard to give life to. He's just the same as one in the earth that have no physical life, to give him a mental resurrection is almost as hard, but nevertheless it's the will of God that we do these things.

Question: I understand that in your view the white race is, mentally, physically, and morally inferior, is that correct?

Messenger: Well, according to the creation of them, they came from another one.

Question: The grafting?

Messenger: Yes sir. And there is...

Question: A watered down version...

Messenger: That's right it reduces it. I don't say we can take him as he is today, this product that has now been robbed, and to try matching him with the white man, no. His slave has been reduced too, you know, a very weak state now. I don't mean him at all. We mean that one that has not been touched by the white man's civilization. But these that have been touched are also weak physically. No, I don't even have that one in mind.

BACKGROUND OF THE MESSENGER'S ROOTS

Question: Is your own individual racial background entirely black?

Messenger: Original before the creation of the white man, we don't have no knowledge of any other colors.

Question: No, I mean you individually, as an individual?

Messenger: An individual, what now?

Question: Person, saying you, is your own individual racial background, you as a person, entirely as a black man?

Messenger: Well, my parents was mixed by white slave-masters, my grandmother, my father's mother was half and half. Her father was white.

Question: Your great grandfather?

Messenger: No sir, my grandfather not my great grandfather, my father's mother.

Question: I see, you mean...

40

Messenger: Not my father's father, just my father, my father whom I am from.

Question: In other words your grandfather was white?

Messenger: My grandfather in this instant, on my grandmothers side, that would be a great grandfather.

Question: Oh, great grandfather

Messenger: Yes sir. Was white.

Question: It's been such a racial melting pot, a racial nationalistic melting pot in the United States is very.... I have to tell you my own racial background is partially, partially mixed. And I think a great number of us do. You have that particular racial background and many don't know it.

Messenger: Well in slavery time, according to slavery history that I have gotten a hold to, and I have gotten a hold to some mighty dusty looking old books. What I mean they're pretty old. This took place when the slave-master wanted to produce lots of slaves. He put himself in to try to make some slaves, then he took all the children and sold them off. According to his own writing that's what he said. And so, I know my own grandmother was half and half, and she looked it and acted it. And so she was used by her father as a slave and her own mother was sold too. She still was a slave and her brother, her half brother who was a Senator once in Georgia, stayed in Georgia, but she didn't talk about it. He

41

was her half brother down, but they knew each other. She goes and visits every now and then, but as I said, she looked like what she was; therefore, she was easy to pass it on. I think the slave-masters made a pretty bad job of going to work to get wealth out of human beings. They did the wrong thing; they should not have mixed their own blood in slaves like that, because that is also a mockery against them too, you know.

Question: Well the whole idea of slavery is a mark against them I believe.

Messenger: Well it is...

Question: The thought of anyone thinking of owning somebody, this is...

Messenger: Another human being as a slave, that's a wicked thing to do, plus the whole world have been against it for a long time, and today, they're trying to get away from it and every now and then you run into a small segment of it still being practiced.

Question: Are there any major misconceptions about the Nation of Islam in North America, do you feel should be cleared up? What are the major public misunderstandings in your view?

Messenger: Well, I think it's all major, because in the first place, the number one place, it is neglecting the time that these things should take place, and when a man is ignorant of the time of such things, then he is out and doing everything, you can't tell him nothing. And so, it's a major thing throughout the whole entire history of this work. It is misunderstanding, that is the number one thing that is causing, well, I wouldn't say that it isn't causing no progress, because progress is being made right on, but there is other little things that is hindering us. I should not use this word, hindered, because it only, in some instances like prosecution. We don't fight it to much, because since it is written and prophesied that God will take care of it. It only spreads it most time, when the believer is arrested and sent to prison, that spreads it. Pretty soon, he has lots of converts around him secretly. Many times, the secret is due to the fact that it is not liked by the guards and the warden of the prison, they keep it within themselves.

MUSLIMS IN PRISON

Question: You know I did a program on prisons in California, and found that it is a very popular movement in some prisons, and some of the prisons in California discourage, and try, and really try and not have people following this faith. Others utilize it, they figure it's a good thing, it helps....

Messenger: Well, it does not make bad prisoners at all, the guards and the warden have a much more easier time trying to keep under control Muslims than he does non-Muslims, because Muslims know that they are suppose to obey the law. Muslims is not going to try to break and run from the prison houses, he's not going to do that, or make an escape, he's not going to attack the guard or try to free himself and others, he's not going to do that.

Question: This is a person, if he's a true convert, you know, I wonder sometimes some of the fellows when they initially pick this up in prison don't fully, probably don't fully understand the entire methods that is used. Followers sometimes get off on something that doesn't.....

Messenger: Yes, well, that stands true when they first start, they're sometimes like, we use the saying, like fish out of water, jumping around, but they soon become, calm and natural, but when they're around some of the older Muslims of the faith then they are kept in check when they first become converts, and that's why we have in Virginia, the law in Virginia, the government gave me the freedom to have a minister go there and visit them, and now there is four hundred of them there in that prison and they don't have no trouble with them.

Question: It's a very interesting thing to me that your among the, among the teachings, among your followers, the natural responsibility and family responsibility are very important aspects and I noticed in reading your paper which I have quite a number of times now, there are many men who got in the Muslim teaching and then feel that this has helped them in establishing there own businesses and things of this nature which they thought before they weren't able to do.

Messenger: You pretty much answered it right. Now here again is the thing: if we were left just alone. I think that to be something that God did not intend, in these prison places. They won't permit me to go and talk with them; well, I understand. If I were permitted, I could probably have prisoners, that is going to prison of my people, very easy to get along with, because I served myself four years in prison. They didn't have no trouble with me and my followers, because I was there, never no trouble in my life in Michigan.

Question: In talking to Bernard Cushmeer, am I pronouncing his last name correctly, Cushmeer?

Messenger: Cushmeer, yes sir.

Question: I was talking to Bernard Cushmeer, I went over I think he sent to you the general offer on the documentary and types of things we're asking for, said that he felt that if it would be possible to secure permission to use some of your films which are available in Atlanta, in Atlanta. And so he suggested that I contact, that I write to Chicago, yeah he told me to write to Chicago which I did, and I haven't heard back from him yet, is there anyone else you would suggest that I should contact in regard to bill some of these films of some of your activities?

Messenger: No sir, I don't know anyone else, myself, unless I contact the National Secretary. I would like you to give me a film from this. We can help. I think within myself, this is a better discussion than I made last time with the educational party from New York. I would love to have a film of this movie and then help.

Questioner: Alright, I'll request that at the station; I can't personally say yes because it's not mine to give away, but I will tell the station ...

Messenger: They don't have to give it the brother, will buy it.

Questioner: Well I think, I'll put it this way, almost always when we work very closely with somebody, we do, yes, make available ....

Messenger: Oh yes sir, because there is yet much work probably ahead. You might want to film some more in the future, but I'm not asking the company to give me these things, which they have to go through a little expenses and everything, the machine, and the workmen, and what not, but if you want to put a price on it I will buy them then and I don't ask them to pay me for my time to sit and talk with you.

Questioner: Yes of course, I understand.

Messenger: No, no. If they would let me have the film so we too could use it for our own references. Sometimes misunderstanding comes up and is charged with saying this or saying that; well then, we could get the films and say, "Here it is, see for yourself." After you have gone through the film and put the pictures and everything on it, I will buy a copy of it.

Question: Are there any historical photographs available anywhere of your movement? Are there any historical photographs of early Mosques, or of Master Fard Muhammad, for example, are they available anywhere?

Messenger: I don't know whether that they would let them go or not, but maybe they are someplace. Whether or not you could get a hold to them, I wouldn't promise it.

Question: I'll try. I'll see if I can get the District Commissioner to work on that aspect and maybe he could make a few inquiries about it. Alright sir, is there anything else you would like to add to our discussion before I leave, I certainly appreciate the time that you took.

Messenger: Oh that's alright I don't think I have anything in mind now but dinner.

Questioner: You know, I didn't plan to take nearly this much of your time but I got so personally interested.

Messenger: I'm glad that you think it was that, I'm glad to talk with you.

Questioner: To me it was a most interesting interview; I must say that you're a most different person than I expected to meet.

Messenger: In what way?

Questioner: Well....

Messenger: I'm not violent, I'm not violent. (laughing)

Questioner: I have never talked to any religious leader before, especially the absolute head of this organization. I've talked to lots of people in Christian church and so on, and I always found them a little bit stuffy which you're not at all. You're very personal and easy going, but what I had been expecting ordinarily from religious leaders is, some that's a little bit stuffy, and a little difficult to talk to sometimes....

Messenger: Well....

Questioner: Or pretentious.

Messenger: Well, we fellows, we don't think we are within our, you know.....

Question: [Races and colors]

Messenger: The color or the races are people, and Islam is religion. When we say the people of Islam, we mean of that religion or that duty to God, and when we refer to the color of the various people of Earth, we are referring to races and nations as they're called: Such as brown, yellow, red colors, they're all from the same source or the same father, the black man; he has that in him. The white color, it's a color, and

48

according to the teachings of Master Fard Muhammad, to Whom Praise is due, God in Person, we call white the fifth color from black and the final color of black. It's not anymore part of the other four; it's completely to itself; it's independent now to itself.

Question: Is it something, which, though it emerged from the others, it is rather completely separate? It is so different, it is no longer the same as the others?

Messenger: Its root is from the first, the black , but it has now been taken completely from that and within itself it's independent.

CAN WHITE PEOPLE BECOME MUSLIMS?

Question: Now Islam, can white people become Muslims?

Messenger: Not by nature. They can't, because Islam means a person that is actually, by nature, born that, with that quality, divine belief, and submissive to that divine will, and by nature they are capable of just being just that people that is of the will of God and easily obey His will.

Question: You mentioned to me earlier, that Mr. Fard was part white?

Messenger: He was part white, He was. When we go into this particular question, which must be gone into, and which is now gone into today, if the answers to the questions has always been there, but the answers has not always been there.

Question: The question has always been there, but not the answers?

Messenger: Due to the fact that the correct answer would interfere with something, or with the god of this world; therefore, the correct answer, direct answer, has not been given but to a few people, in order to allow the god of this world to rule. As they were given this time to rule, and going into such question is really who is who, who are you, and who am I. It's the kind of an answer or question, that when answered, truthfully, it may make some people feel good and may make some people feel bad. We're talking to scholars and scientist on this same question and answer. We don't expect to meet with opposition, because they understand so much of it anyway, and maybe they understand or feel like they understand the whole. The coming of a God today has meanings, which the average person cannot accept and really I would not teach what I am answering or rather talking with you now, I wouldn't answer the question in the public.

Question: You wouldn't give this answer that you're giving now, even to the members of the Nation of Islam?

Messenger: Not unless I thought that those present would be expecting such, that have moved up to such answer, and

50

maybe I could give them.....

Question: Or prepared them?

Messenger: Yes sir. They are qualified to receive such a thing, and even take it. And the others maybe you could give an answer, and some of those that is not qualified yet will not understand. And you have to bring him up to it like we have to bring a child up from alphabets to read. And so, this is the meticulous thing that I'm saying to you in words that we're entering into this kind of field. According to the knowledge that I have received, been given from Allah, it is not something that we could play with. The answer to the question would take us into the circle of God, and how His aims come about, and how and why we are calling such and such person God, and such and such act of God. We are getting at the root of it, and it's being kept such secret for so long that some people is rather happy to receive the answer to it, and some people is yet confused and do not understand; therefore, it should not be said, given just openly, but only to a people that you're going to school into it, or to people who already have the knowledge of it.

Question: Let me say I appreciate your confidence in me to answer this question and....

Messenger: I thank you. Since you're are a member of this group I assume, and your people being also, you know, people that are religious people, who have received this kind of teaching indirectly anyway and are followers of the first

51

prophet who we call Musa, or Moses. In the Bible we say Moses, and in the Holy Qur'an we call him by the Arab language. Musa or Moses of the first religious scripture from whom, the people of this particular age, not the first of their world, but the first of this age, who are part of the history of the people of the Earth and they lived this, and they're under this and they received this and they received that. Now having knowledge of the prophets and their prophecies and sayings, it is badly true that Israel as we call them, Jews today - as we know the origin of that name - plenty of your people are pretty close to the Arab religion, as it's referred to, but it's not the Arab religion anymore than anyone else's. Only, they have been people accepted in trying to live it. We have plenty of them on the history, or on record, rather than Islam, have tried to obey and follow the law and teaching that Moses had given to them.

DO YOU CONSIDER JEWS AS WHITE PEOPLE?

Question: But you would regard these people of Israel as white?
In a kind of special position in some way, because they have tried to follow the precepts of the law?

Messenger: That's right, they made themselves a little different from the others who did not; therefore, they have been blessed in the past, and they are blessed above the others who are not followers of the Muslim's teachings.

Question: You may recall when I asked this question that related to the manner of race and color. I had asked you whether a white man can become a Muslim, and had said to me by nature he could not?

Messenger: He could not.

Question: He could not. And then I asked you well, about Mr. Fard whom you told me....

Messenger: I am coming up to that.
Questioner: I'm sorry.

Messenger: That's exactly why, now since I said that this Israel or the scholars of Israel have this in their prophecy of the coming of a last man, and the nature in which he must come; this man that must come and must go after that which is lost, He must be a prepared man in order to fit the job well, He must be prepared, He must be part of both.

Question: Both what, I'm sorry?

Messenger: Both people, black and white, because....

Question: Your speaking of the Jew?

Messenger: Well, I'm speaking of white generally, and black generally, and He has to be part if we're making a study, or if we have to study the necessity of the Man and His work that He is to do. We must have both, because here He judges one and He takes another. He judges both and He must get among both. His first work of getting among the one that He comes among to judge. He must get this freedom to get among them in such ways that they will never be able to discover Him as being just what He really is.

Question: May I put it this way, and please tell me if I'm correct, or incorrect that this person who is prophesied to come among the lost-found Tribe of Shabazz, must be a part of both races in order to teach the one race, the black race and to be a Muslim, and also to be a part of the white race so that He may travel and move among the white race to understand them, to learn from them, or to learn about them I should say, and to be able to judge them. And for this reason He must be acceptable....

Messenger: Disguised in such manner.

Question: In such manner to be in both races?

Messenger: That's right.

Question: And this is the part of the teaching which you say you are revealing to me now because I am Jewish and I am a scholar, is that correct?

Messenger: Yes, because you are of the people that the

scripture was given to, and not to the Christian people. You are the people, therefore, I feel free to talk with you because you already have it.

Question: You would not, may I ask, reveal this to your own followers?

Messenger: Yes I'm trying to teach them, but not as direct as you because you already understand.

Question: Not everybody is prepared to receive this understanding, you feel it should only be given to those who are ready for it?

Messenger: Well, you feel free to talk with person who knows what you're talking about than you do a person who don't know what you're talking about.

ARE TURKISH PEOPLE MUSLIMS?

Question: Yes. There's no need to talk if it isn't going to be understood? Obviously. I see. Again, on the question of color let me ask you about the people called the Turks, now they are Muslims, and I think that your sons, Akbar, after your trip to the middle east reported on the strength of Islam in Turkey. Now would you regard them as white people as.....

Messenger: They are white people.

Question: They are white. And yet they are Muslims?

Messenger: They are Muslims as far as the belief is concerned; they are not Muslim by nature, but they are Muslims by faith.

Question: I see. Well let me explore a little bit with you this difference between nature and faith. Do you mean by this, a man can adopt the religion of Islam, that is, he can do the things that are required externally, or superficially on the outside to be a Muslim, but that there is something yet in him which makes it impossible for him to be a Muslim if he is white?

Messenger: If he is of Israel. I will give it..., We will talk plain. If he is of Israel, or the people of Yakub, he could not say truthfully that he is by nature this, but the people other than Yakub's people are Muslims by nature, because they are of the people of that particular originator of the Heaven and the Earth; therefore, they're direct, but this is an off-branch and is not the direct.

Question: And let me see if I express it correct. Before the time of Yakub, there were black people, red people, yellow people, and brown people?

Messenger: I don't say all of these colors.

THE MAKING OF THE WHITE RACE

Question: There was black people who were the original, then came the others, the whites came last. Now all of these, the original people, the black people, and all the other colored people, were by nature could be Muslim?

Messenger: Yes.

Question: If they wanted to?

Messenger: Yes sir up to the white man.

Question: Up to, not including the white man?

Messenger: Not including the white man.

Question: Now these, then came Yakub, and he created something different, although it came originally....

Messenger: I don't want you to get confused there. Where you are confusing me in your question. I don't want you to confuse me in your question, and I don't want to confuse you in answering something that you are not actually asking, here is the thing of it: Yakub did not make ahead these colors, brown, yellow, and red, situated off on the planet Earth as they are today before you, but these are colors produced in

57

getting to the last color. They have not always been. We have not always had independent brown, yellow, and red race.

Question: I see, these were stages on the way to the white race?

Messenger: That's right.

Question: And Yakub came and made the final stage?

Messenger: Yes, he produced the set up to produce his man and produced these too. At that same time they come this way. We don't have readings, or rather He didn't teach me that these colors took place, and was living independently as nations before Yakub's work of producing a new man.

Question: I see, now let me understand it then. The time Yakub came, the black man only existed, then he produced, in the process of producing the white man, he produced the other colors, but when he produced the other colors, but when he reached the white he had something that was rather different from all the others.

Messenger: He had a completely different man.

Question: Completely different thing?

Messenger: That's right.

Question: And these others, were all by nature, Muslim, or...

58

Messenger: Until he got....

Question: Until he got to the white man?

Messenger: That's right.

Question: Who was no longer by nature Muslim? So the white could then adopt the faith or the religion of Islam without being by nature a Muslim?

Messenger: Right.

Questioner: This is as I understand it now.

Messenger: When we say that the white man can't be a Muslim, it don't mean that he can't believe it, it means that by nature he cannot believe it.

Question: Because he came later?

Messenger: Well he's a completely different man.

Question: Completely different being?

Messenger: Yes sir, altogether. He's not the same being. I would like to say this, according to his teaching, the first two hundred years of his grafting he produced a brown race.

Question: I see. This is why you say the white race was six hundred years in birth?

Messenger: That's right.

Question: The first two hundred years he produced a brown race?

Messenger: He produced a complete brown race, he had no more black.

Question: I see and then his second two hundred years?

Messenger: His process of grafting had erased the black, it was in two hundred years; it was in two hundred years he had erased the black and had a brown race and his process of keeping apart the black from the browner, or yellow, or whiter, until he got to the last stage. Once in effect, it was so strong that there was no more black after two hundred years, and even after four hundred years, there was no more brown. The brown had also been erased in his process of grafting. His grafting was reaching for white; he was going to take this germ into it's last stage. The black germ into the last stage would be white.

Question: In other words then, he arrived on Earth when there was only the black race?

Messenger: Only the black race.

Question: He created the brown out of the black, and the black was erased?

Messenger: That's right.

Question: Then he had only the brown, that took two hundred years, then in the next two hundred years he created the red, and then the brown and the black one no longer.....

Messenger: Or yellow yes sir, and then....

Question: Then he created the yellow, in the last two hundred years, and then there were no longer red, brown, or black?

Messenger: Remember, some of these, I'm not saying that they did not exist, but he did not have them. He did not have them.

Question: He didn't have these materials to work with?

Messenger: To work with, no.

Question: They lived, I mean black people continued to exist?

Messenger: We have them today, and they came from that work, but they did not exist in his work, I mean to say, they were not his people yet. He's yet reaching for his people.

Question: Yes. His people are the white people

Messenger: They're the white people.

Question: And there was no, when he reached the brown,

61

there was no black, when he reached the red, there was no brown, when he reached the yellow, there was no red, and when he reached the white there was no yellow, and so there was nothing of the original in the white?

Messenger: Nothing.

Question: And this represents the..., and this took the six hundred year process.

Messenger: And that's when his work was finished. And that was his complete aim and purpose.

A NEW BOOK

Question: Now, let me ask you, I have read in something that you wrote, there will be a new Holy Book to supersede, or to replace both the Bible, and Qur'an.

Messenger: Of today.

Question: Of today. This will be a new Holy Book. Now when will this book come, and who will produce it, or can you tell me anything about it?

Messenger: Well what's in the book is not yet revealed. But this same Man, Master Fard Muhammad, is the very same One that this book will come from. And He said that He has already wrote the book, but He's not ready to give it to the world.

Question: Is there a sign or some indication when He will be ready?

Messenger: I would not say even that which I think or have knowledge of, It's a good question. That is a book that takes us on the other side.

Question: Because it's not, it's not of the Earth? So you wouldn't have knowledge, or wouldn't want to speak?
Messenger: I don't have the knowledge of it's contents, and I wouldn't speak on what I do have knowledge of, or to cover anything like that because it's up on the other side, in the future.

IS THE BIBLE WRONG OR MISLEADING?

Question: Now you have said also that the Bible in some respects is wrong and misleading?

Messenger: Yes sir. According to the teachings of Almighty God in the person of Master Fard Muhammad to me, they have misplaced, or added in and out of the book.

Question: But it's in that editing they have made mistakes?

Messenger: Yes sir.

Question: Deliberate would you say?

Messenger: In fact, I would say, according to the Qur'an, absolutely deliberate. On certain truths.

Question: Now have you, or did Master Fard tell the followers exactly what parts of the Bible one may accept, and exactly what parts of the Bible are untrue?

Messenger: No. He did not detail it, no sir. He didn't detail it, because it's to be understood, you can't detail out to the people. You would have to go all over the Bible and give them lessons, and school the person to detail it, but the work is made much shorter by giving a man the knowledge of it. It's the divine knowledge of it, and that makes the work much shorter.

Question: Yes, if you take out the parts that are misleading from the Bible, you have something which is rather brief, as compared with the original.

Messenger: Well that's a quite a bit of work to go and take it out and separate what is not right.

Question: Do you know that yourself?

HISTORY OF THE NATION OF ISLAM

Messenger: To have you understand it as you see it; say for an instance, there is much said that means truth, but no one knows exactly how to interpret it, and the true interpretation of it, if known, would give us the knowledge, you know, knowledge of what's really is written.

Question: I actually don't have to many more questions I want to ask you, I don't..., it will take too long, if you will just permit me to...

Messenger: Go right ahead.

Question: I know I have taken more time than you have planned, and I'm grateful to you for giving it to me.

Messenger: Well, your questions is so plentiful, you know, and what should be said, and since you're a great and wise scholar, I do think that these answers should be given to you.

Questioner: Thank you very much.

Messenger: Since we are meeting on the horizon, we must either keep going around it, or we must divide our travel.

Question: Well, let me just say, since trying to understand the teachings of Mr. Fard, and yourself....

Messenger: I see that you must be interested.

Question: I've devoted, I began in 1961 on this, and I had a whole summer planned to do a certain kind of research, but when I began to find out and read about this movement, that shot my whole schedule completely awry, and I spent the entire summer of 1961 trying to find out about it, and this is when I first met Minister Malcolm X in Trenton at that time.

Messenger: I hope you sell me a copy of your first book (laughing).

Question: I wouldn't sell it to you, I would certainly present you with a copy. In a sense, I have been preparing now for two years to talk with you on these things, and trying to understand them as much as I was able to first before I, in coming to talk with you. I might also say that I was very, what really set me off to study this whole thing was your claim, or your statement that the original religion of the Negroes, the Black man, is Islam. And that posed the question in my mind as to what was the religion of the black slaves brought to this country? And I began to investigate the records and study this question, and this is what set me off and ruined my schedule for the summer. Well anyway, that's just a bit of personal history. Let me ask you one, two questions about words and pronunciation. I asked you about the origin of the word Shabazz, and you answered that question in the way that you wanted to, let me ask you, you pronounce the word Qur'an, is that correct for the Holy Book of the Moslem?

QUR'AN VERSUS KORAN, MUSLIM VERSUS MOSLEM, OR MUHAMMAD VERSUS MOHAMMED

Messenger: Well you know, we just uses the Q, and the average English speaker uses K in the spelling.

Question: You use the Q in your various ways is with the K?

Messenger: It is with most scholars to say Qur'an that to say Koran. They say Koran.

Question: I'm speaking rather of the W when you say Qur'an, is this the common way it is pronounced among your followers, or is this a....

Messenger: Qur'an is the common way.

Question: Would you regard that as the correct way?

Messenger: Well, according to the sound, and the translation of the Arab, they uses mostly as probably you know the Q for spelling it instead of K in the translation.

Question: It's the R you say, they say Qur'an?

Messenger: Yes sir. Qur'an.

Question: Whereas I hear you say Qu'wan (W pronunciation)

Messenger: Well that's the sound you know we say, Qur'an. Qur'an, and some scholars they have heard pronounce, they say Gu'wan, you know, the sound, it sounds as Qur'an.

Question: Some people who speak Arabic would say Qur'an, and others would say Gur'an (laughing). Now let me ask you about the difference between, I know that you make a strong distinction between the word Muslim, and the word Moslem as it's often pronounced Moslem?

Messenger: But the meanings is exactly the same thing, the English say Moslem, rather the word Muslim. They mean the same; we say Muslim.

Question: Would you regard it as sacrilegious for example, or blasphemous, or something to say Moslem. Is this not an insult for example for a Muslim to say that? It's simply a matter of incorrect pronunciation?

Messenger: It's just like saying Mohammed, and we say Muhammad, the meanings is the same.

ON RETURNING TO AFRICA

Question: Thank you. I have just two questions and then I'll be finished, I saw the interview that you had with the reporter from the New York Herald Tribune, no the New York Times, I'm sorry, a Mr. Handler. There is an article in the New York Times reporting his interview with you, and you said there according to his report that your first choice would be to return to Africa. Did he report that correctly?

Messenger: That's right, you're referring to separation of the so-called American Negro and his former slave-masters. Yes, we would rather, especially those who believe in Islam, would rather be sent back where we came from, but if we are not given that freedom to return to where we came from, then to provide us a separate place here in order to prevent all of this dissatisfaction. Give us a chance to make a nation out of ourselves or give what we believe would be good for ourself as you have built for your own self. We have centuries here of experience among you that you and I can't get along together in peace. In fact, if we could peacefully get along together, I would want something for myself as you want something for yourself. You have gotten for yourself. I'm in your house. I would like to get out and build me a house of my own, of my own you choosing.

ON VOTING

Question: Now in the past, as I understand you have not urged your followers to vote?

Messenger: No.

Question: Is that correct?

Messenger: No.

Question: Is this, I have read in various places, I don't think anything officially, but I'd like this officially coming from the leaders of the Nation of Islam. What I would like to know, do you plan to urge your people to vote, and to run for office and so on. In other words, do you plan to ask them to take part in political movements in anyway? I don't know if you want to answer that question, but I thought I would like to ask it?

Messenger: Well that depends, but according to looking at the clock of time in this work that I'm doing here, my particular job is just that which is predicted to do. That is to shape a people for self respect and universal recognition. I am not sure whether or not such time will come in my work when we will be preparing for a political setup here in the government of America or not, but just in case we become news here in the government, we would like to have a representative going to the government or in Washington to represent us of our own choosing.

70

Question: You mean a member of the Congress actually, is that what you're referring to?

Messenger: Yes sir. We would like to be represented you know, according to our own.

Question: You're speaking now, not of the so-called American Negro, but you're speaking of the Nation of Islam itself?

Messenger: Well, if we are dominant, whether in numbers or in power, we would include the whole. In fact, I'm not after a few in this manner, I am after the whole. I would like to see the whole represented rightly, and given justice; I want them to be justified, but I do know that it takes qualification to be represented and recognized by the government, and that is what I am trying to do now is to qualify my people to receive recognition in this government, or any other government, wherever we go. We have to be fit for respect of that government.

Questioner: I'm sorry sir, I had only two questions, one more occurred.

Messenger: That's alright.

WAS MR. FARD A MEMBER OF THE NOBLE DREW ALI MOVEMENT?

Question: I have read, Mr. Fard Himself, was He a member of Nobel Drew Ali's movement?

Messenger: No. He was no member....

Question: Or He was a follower or something.....

Messenger: He's independent, He's not a follower of any of them. He's not.

Question: Was He associated in any way with Noble Drew Ali?

Messenger: No.

Question: These reports then so far as you are concerned are incorrect?

Messenger: That's incorrect, that's right. He was no follower of Noble Drew Ali. No, He's no follower of anyone, He's self independent. He's self independent, there's nobody for Him to follow.

Question: There's a book called, <u>They Seek A City</u>, written by Arnab Bantar, and Jack Conroy which stated it could be the case and I just wanted to know from you what you thought of it?

Messenger: But the writer didn't have an understanding, as of so many still writing, don't have good knowledge of what to write on a subject, but they want to hurry out with something.

ON E. U. ESSIEN-UDOM'S BOOK: <u>BLACK NATIONALISM</u>

Question: Have you read Mr. E.U. Essien-Udom's book?

Messenger: I've read enough of that.

Question: What was your impression of that?

Messenger: Well, he have some good in there, and I could also classify him with the hasty writer. He's to hasty in what he wants to write, and probably would write correctly, but he wants to hurry and get that on the market.

Question: Is there anything written by anybody but a member of the Nation of Islam, would you regard as a good report? As a fair and a correct, reasonably correct report, humanly correct report?

Messenger: Well, the man that you just mentioned.....

Question: Essien?

ON C. ERIC LINCOLN'S BOOK: BLACK MUSLIMS IN AMERICA

Messenger: Yes sir. And also this other writer here in Atlanta.

Question: Eric Lincoln?

Messenger: Yes sir. They both have very good things in it and they have things in it, in there writing, that show undeveloped knowledge of just what's what that I don't detest so, I just classify it as people who want to write.

Question: Well...

THE MESSENGER INTERVIEWS THE INTERVIEWER

Messenger: I would like to ask you some questions (laughing).

Question: I'm sorry, I should have shown more politeness and gratitude.

Messenger: That's alright, but I would like to.

Questioner: I know that you have things to do, and I didn't want to take up more of your time.

Messenger: In your research, and your gathering of knowledge of this particular movement, especially the work and teaching that I'm doing here, since you are of Israel, is this [interview] for the purpose of giving a true side of what is going on here in America among the dark people, or is it for criticism. You may think I should have asked you that in the beginning (laughing). The answer can be yes or no with me, but here is what I'm after: Since the writings of these people, of us, has been partly correct and partly incorrect, that according to the ever changing time and the needs of the time for us, for man, would you say that these movements being made in America among us is foreseen and should be expected, or they're not foreseen or should not be expected. It can't be said that they are not possible because they are.

Questioner: We're here.

Messenger: Yes sir. But how do you look at these movements?

Question: Now when you say this movement, you mean your own movement?

Messenger: I'm including all of what the term, the so-called American Negro seeking something towards self, or a way to independence, or something near to the white man? (separationist or integrationist movements)

Questioner: Well, It's a big question, but I'll try to answer it within a brief way. First as to what I believe, I, and how I feel about these things, I think this is what you want, at least part of your question, is that it?

Messenger: That's right.

Questioner: Well, I feel sympathetic, I think, to what the Negro wants to do in this country, that is to establish himself, to achieve something to overcome the legacy of slavery, and of discrimination, and of exploitation, because I think there's no question that he has been exploited and discriminated against and I would like to see these things corrected, but I think it is not only the Negroes job to do this, I think it is also the white man's job to do this. And I would like to see that come. And so, I sympathize very much with the Negroes who are trying to achieve this, to work among themselves, as well as to convince the white man what needs to be done, and to draw his attention the evils that have been created here. I must add, in all honesty however, that I don't participate very much in these things, it's a matter of one's personality, and one's profession and I myself, as a scholar, prefer to read, and write, and understand, that is, I'm not going to march on Washington and I don't, shall I say....

Messenger: You would like to know the reason why I want to march on Washington?

Questioner: That's right, exactly. I have a great curiosity about human behavior, not only the behavior of American Negroes, because I have studied other groups as well, now as I mentioned earlier, to answer the other question that you asked about what I, about presenting the ideas and the teachings of this movement, I feel that it is my obligation in trying to understand what the people are doing, to report what they think, they are doing, see. I want to put it so that they, I will explain in the best way that I understand what they believe they are doing. At the same time.... go right ahead....

Messenger: Whatever right, we always have our own personal opinions.

Questioner: I do not, however, relinquish my right as a scholar, and as an individual to interpret in my own way, I don't mean this to interpret in hostility, but to interpret what I think it means. This is for example if you ever take a look at this book which I've left with you, you will see that what I try to explain what the Arabs do and think, I try to do that in their own way, in a way which they will accept, they will say yes, this is what we believe, you have described this accurately, then I go on to analyze in my own way what I think is correct or, or what I understand may be quite distinct, but I reserve that right as an independent scholar to do that.

Messenger: Why certainly, why certainly. And now I'm asking you this now, do you think, or what is your conception of the various movements made here. There are two major movements that's being made here: one is for staying with the master, and forcing the master to keep his doors open to them, and the other one is for total separation from the master. Which one of these movements, how do you look at?

Questioner: If I had to say it in twenty words or so, I would say that I understand why Negroes would want to separate, I feel however that that is impossible, and I believe, I disagree with you, I don't believe that the white people and Negroes come from a completely different stock, so to speak, that they have a different origin. I believe that there is one human origin, scientifically and emotionally. I believe this, and so I believe that ultimately that human beings aught to be able to work together and live together, I really would like to see that. As I say however, I can understand why Negroes, some and even all Negroes, would want to separate.

Messenger: But you believe that they all should live together?

Questioner: Yes.

Messenger: If you was questioned on your belief would you accept it?

Questioner: How do you mean?

Messenger: How do you arrive at anything in your belief that you could give to me that would support your belief?

Questioner: Impossible, well, there isn't much evidence that is possible; I think, on certain levels among human beings, there have been from time to time examples of people coming together who have previously fought or one had exploited the other where this was possible, on the other hand, I had the idea of complete separation itself, I find not only difficult to achieve, but also, I say this is also, I sense a defeat of a noble ideal if one were to admit this, see, I understand why people think this way and speak this way, but for me that's an admission of defeat of a human goal.

Messenger: Where do you take me to witness or bear witness to you that this is the human goal for all to live together and mix together with one being the master of the other?

Questioner: I don't believe..., I think that there are people who are leaders, and there are people who are followers. I don't think that there should be masters of anyone.

Messenger: Someone's got to be master, we can't just erase the general laws of nature, we have that working throughout the universe. Even the planets are built upon such laws. The

Creator points this out, we can't erase that, somebody's got to be the leader.

Questioner: Islam is equality, I mean what do we mean by equality then?

Messenger: You know how we look at things. If you say that the races should be merged and live together, and not be separated, I'm asking you, where do you find it, where can you point to me in the past history where such ever happened and it was a success?

Questioner: It's happened considerably. I don't know what we mean by success, but racial mixture has been going on in the world for thousands of years.

Messenger: I know that, I know that, ever since you been here. In the south it has been going on, it's your fathers idea. This was in the work of your people, not in ours. It was the fathers ideas of your people to mix them and yet made themselves dominant. We hinted at this some time ago going into relive the core of the thing. Maybe we may start pulling away poles apart, but still, we must come to the knowledge of truth in the thing and to do justice in it. Does it look reasonable, does it look intelligent for you and I to merge in together and you are yet dominate?

Questioner: Not dominate.

Messenger: One of us got to dominate the others.

Questioner: Why must it be that all the people who are dominate will be of one color, and all the people who are not dominate will be of the other color? All I'm saying is why don't they be people of each color among the dominant?

Messenger: We have it like that, it was like that when you started dominating the world, we had brown, yellow, and red, dominating one sphere to themselves, and others on to themselves.

Questioner: There's one difficulty in trying to explore one another's opinions on these things and that is while I respect religions, all peoples religions....

Messenger: This is not the point, the question here is not based upon a religion, it's based upon people and just forget about religion.

Questioner: Well...

Messenger: You are telling me the way you see it, that it would be better for us to try to live here and try and make ourselves social members or citizens along with the white man, instead of trying to go for ourselves and make for ourselves an independent government for ourselves as the white man? But your picture is that your best bet is to try and make friendship with this people, and let them teach and train you how they will respect you as a member among themselves, but they still will own the country, they still will be the dominant rulers and not us, they can't say that they will strike a dividing line. If you have said in the beginning, that it would be nice that you both live together and become neighbors and act like neighbors or friends instead of separating, but one should have a room here, and the other one should have a room over there. This is what I'm asking: if I can't go to my own home, will you give me a room in your own home that I can call my own room and not just a room in your house that you can evict me anytime you desire. It depends on my act, but if I'm given a room, then I own that room and will be the landlord of my own room. If you are to help me to get the room started, in building the room, creating the room, supporting the room, for a length of time, I have to show you, that I'm worthy of it on the conditions between you and I.

Questioner: I understand what you're saying, but my attitude would be this, I would say, I would not favor giving to a whole group this idea of a room, I would say that every individual no matter what race or color he may be, has the right to have this room of his own, to have the right to do what he is capable of as an individual.

Messenger: I think you are misunderstanding. I don't mean just the Muslim have....

Questioner: I understand, I mean all the Negroes.

Messenger: The entire darker people in America.

Questioner: I don't believe that. I don't think that the Jews should be given an opportunity as a group of Jews. I don't believe that the Poles or the Christians or the Methodist, and I don't believe that the Negroes aught to be given that opportunity as a group of Negroes to stay together, live together, have this room that they could call their own. I believe that every individual who is prepared in his own way, as an individual, intellectually, emotionally, psychologically, should have the absolute right to achieve everything he can achieve, and that nobody would stand in his way except in the ordinary manners of the laws of the land which apply to everybody, not just to this individual, I think that and I believe that there are many Negroes, and even to it that way already sounds condescending, but I see no reason so. Negroes are not already prepared to live fully, completely equalized in their own way to the extent of their individual capacities, and their wealth even, and their intellectual ability allows them.

Messenger: Yes.

Questioner: And that should be done on an individual basis for every individual who can do it.

Messenger: Yes.

Questioner: This is my own belief.

Messenger: They're among us, people that is capable of starting an independent government for themselves and their entire people. But they needs help, support. But, that same person trying now to become an equal member of the superior people that he's already enslaved under, I'm trying to get at that point, you're not advising me, which you could not. You could not advise me to leave America, that would be against the friendship of America and yourself. I'm not even asking for that. I'm asking this, to show me this truthfully, whether or not the idea that the two, this is on the table now, one group is working for separation, total separation, while the other group is working for a total emerging in. What makes sense, if that people has already been enslaved for four hundred years under the same people and are suffering injustice at the hand of that people at the very moment, what makes sense: to try now to ask the master to change his mind and allow the man to live in more better comfortable peace with you. If he want to go since you have freed him, you said you freed him...

Questioner: Yes.

Messenger: If he want to go from you even the public should go on from you.

Questioner: Because things change from time to time, because if Negroes would deny that, for example, twenty years ago the things that they are demanding today, they would be cut down in the streets.

Messenger: Yeah they would.

Questioner: Much more often than they would, they are still cut down in the streets, but they would be cut down much more than they are today. Now how do we account for that, why is it that the white people are willing now more to grant the demands of some Negroes than they were twenty years ago.

Messenger: Because of the time that has arrived.

Questioner: Well, I hope that the time will arrive when they will be able to live together in peace.

Messenger: But you wasn't able to do it, your people was not able to do it. The Japanese and the Chinese, and the other people or the races of the people was not able to do it.

Questioner: England and France fought for many hundreds of years, now they don't fight anymore. Germany and France just fought and I think and hope they will be able to be overcome. I don't know any other solution myself you see, I cannot see the mechanism of any other solution. I'm not saying by the way that the future of the Negro is rosy and that everything will be solved in this country, I'm not saying that by any means. I'm only saying that so far as I can see, this is the road that it has to take, it may not ever go far enough on that road, but that's the road that it must take.

Messenger: Of trying to solve the problem of the two races' living....

Questioner: I don't see it as the two races living together, and coming together, I think that that is very, very far off, for example, look at Jews....

Messenger: They can't do it.

Questioner: Well, they have been doing it. I mean certainly all of the light colored people in this country, that is, the mixed dark and light people are the consequence of the people co-habituating, I mean that's quite clear that has happened.

Messenger: That's what we're getting after now, you have had the freedom to discolor my people, but we haven't had that kind of freedom to discolor your people. You're to intelligent for that, but we have been so dumb, and too weak to oppose you, and now since we are not strong enough yet to oppose you, we want to go from you to stop you from destroying us.

Questioner: I think that, yes I understand, let me put it this way, even the road that I regard as the proper one, for the relationship of the Negroes and the whites of this country, I think even that road will produce separation, because I believe that as the Negro develops his own demands, and his own ideas, and wants to be his own master, even though he preaches, or even though he, for example, Martin Luther King and others may preach integration, they are really separating, whether they talk integration or they don't talk integration they are really separating to a certain extent.

Messenger: To a certain extent is right.

Questioner: They are really separating no matter what they say they are doing. And I think that this kind of separation is the kind, is essential to the ultimate coming together of the

86

two groups on the basis of equality. But to hold out the idea of separation forever, and for eternity, I mean this is something that I can't accept. Now it may only be emotionally that I can't accept it, or I don't know whatever it may be, but that's the way I feel, I think that, for example, I think that all these terms that we use, we draw these distinctions too sharply, I don't think that those who preach separation preach ultimate and absolute separation, I think those who preach integration, are not really preaching ultimate integration, I think that those who talk about non-violence are not always non-violent, and are always really involved in violence whether they create it or not, but they are frequently involved in violent matters; whereas, those who say they are against non-violence are not necessarily always involved in violence. So I think that these terms, in a way, imprison us, and make it difficult for us to understand what's going on in the world.

Messenger: But you know why, that it creates violence, even for us to preach non-violence, and even act on the principle of it, you know why it arises, it's due to your brother that don't want to accept anything like justice towards us. He makes the trouble as he has always made it. Because he have a free horse here, that he have hired for a long time, and the horse now may rise his feet, and kick up. He don't want to be harnessed by the same rider, he want to go without the rider's saddle. And so, this master, he still wants to force the horse, though the horse is not bothering the master, he just wants to graze over here in a pasture himself. So this is the truth on that, and this is the truth on our part, and this is the truth on the time, divine time of this matter. Divinely we have to recognize the fact that the prophets could not have lied when they spoke and wrote of a separation of us. They could not have lied, because so much of it is being fulfilled. It has been talked and written about, not a hundred years ago, but thousands of years ago. Why should we expect today to deceive those prophet's writing or their inspiration that they received concerning these times anymore than they wrote and predicted accurately about war. We cannot just say that he's a liar about the so-called Negro and his master.

Questioner: Well, when you put it to me that way you see, then I must say to you what I began to say earlier, and that is that I cannot accept religious teachings of this kind.

Messenger: You cannot accept the religious teaching of this kind?

Questioner: I don't mean that I cannot accept your religious teaching, I don't mean only yours, I mean anybody's. See, I don't interpret life and the causes of things in those terms. You see, this is why I have been able to say, I am not, I don't mean to be disrespectful, but I'm sure you're aware, many people have said, is this movement really Islam, or is this movement really a religion, and what is it. Well, I believe it is a religion, and I honestly believe it is a religion as much as anything is a religion. And if it's confusing, well so is much other religions are confusing too. And I don't think that you can read the Qur'an, or you can read the old testament, or the new testament, in a way that you can read any straight forward account of what is happening, there are many confusing things in there, and I have written something which I hope will be published, but it is not yet published. I believe that if people spend, if the best minds of a society were to spend two thousand years on the teachings of Mr. Fard, and of your teachings, they would make the same kind of build up, the same sort of literature that two or three or five thousand years has built up on the basis of the old, or the new testament, but having said this, I must add that I am not committed to that as an individual, you see, because I cannot accept what somebody prophesied five thousand years ago.

Messenger: Even though it has come to past?

Questioner: Well, I believe that prophesies are of the nature that you can always find evidence for when they have come to past. Human nature, human life is such, if you will excuse me, human life is such that if you predict evil, and shame, and despair, and terrible things, sooner or later you will be right, because human beings are always producing these things.

Messenger: You are telling me then that you're an atheist, and that you don't put any credit to what is formerly said or predicted.....

Questioner: I put credit on those things if I can see the evidence and the reasoning behind them. Not if somebody tells me that this comes from God, because anybody can have visions, anybody can say he has visions I should say.

Messenger: Here is the thing: Because you looked up, I

don't look up for God, I look here for God, I don't look up for God, because there's nothing up there to look for. God is here (pointing to himself), we are Gods and we don't look up for the God.

Questioner: Well I would agree to that extent.

Messenger: But, if a wiser character among us proves that he's wiser, and has more wisdom in power, then we just have to respect him as being of such right?

Questioner: I agree.

Messenger: Yes sir. Well then when we don't respect him being such, we are called infidels or atheist for not doing so, we got to....

Questioner: That doesn't bother me, I'm not concerned, I'm not worried about that.

Messenger: But you do say to me in words, that you don't believe what one have said yesterday concerning God, if it was referring to God. And God only means we could consider it, as a word meaning power and force, that which is superior to inferior on the thing.

Questioner: If that's what you mean by it then I would agree yes. I believe in the superior over the inferior. I believe in the wise over the foolish.

Messenger: We've got to, we've got to. Alright well that's all it means.

Questioner: Well then we stand agreed on that.

Messenger: You say that maybe you wouldn't believe that Yakub made this six thousand years ago. Maybe you could tell me that, but I have proof that he did this because of his works. You could say maybe this don't mean anything at all; yet, we shouldn't do these things, but you didn't find them merged together and functioning. You're giving a picture of what you think today. If it had been so, maybe the same general laws would work successfully for us today.

Questioner: Look at the question of, take Jews alone, I have met Jews in various parts of the world who are dark, who are as dark as Negroes, as dark as dark Negroes, who has features which are considerably different from my own....

Messenger: May I say, pardon me for cutting in, may I say to you, do you consider the word even Jew as a race or nation?

Questioner: It's very difficult to say....

Messenger: Oh no sir. It's kind of like you're getting up to evade that.

Questioner: It's all kinds of things, I'm not going to evade it, I'm not saying that you can't call it a race, you can't call it a nation, you can't call it only a religion, you've got to call it, it's many things, it's different things to different people. Now to

91

the Jews in Israel, it means one thing, now to Jews outside it may mean another, and among the Jews outside of Israel, it maybe means different things, just the other day only, I read in the news paper, a man who is a Christian priest became a citizen of Israel, and calls himself a Jew of the Christian faith because he says in Israel to be a Jew is to be a member of a nation, not a member of a religion. And he is a member of the Jewish nation, living in Israel, and a citizen of that country, but he is also a member of the Christian faith.

Messenger: We have to refer to these things according to the fundamental truth of them and the principles in which they have fashioned upon. Israel, we know is the whole of the white race, when we say Israel, it's the whole of the white race. And we do know according to the study and the nature of the people today, they are a grafted people, we know that, and your scientists admit the same. Well now then, we cannot say that anymore than the symbolic lessons given to us in the Bible of these grafted hogs from the original hogs for instance. We cannot say we can over look the fact that we can take the graft and the original and produce or rather keep them together and leave one as a slave to the other after knowledge, you can't, you just can't do that. That's against the very law of nature for such, and if we are asking freedom to move here, we're doing nothing more than what you have once did according to the history of your race, it is nothing more than right that we try man, this is the nature of people, if I can't get along with you I'll leave you. That's the nature of people. To force me to get along with you against my will, will not produce peace among you and I, no, because deep within I am still, probably poles apart from your way, or, we say, thinking or doing.

Questioner: Well, I would agree with that to this extent, I don't think that people ought to be forced to do things that are against their nature or against their will, and what I mean for example, that if the Negro want's to live among other Negroes that he shouldn't be forced to live in a white neighborhood. I mean, I regard that as a silly kind of product of this whole civil rights movement with a certain amount of confusion attached to it. I don't believe that if a Negro prefers to marry another Negro that he should be called..., that something's wrong with him for not wanting to marry a white person. I don't believe that, I believe that if Negroes want to live among themselves, they should be free to do so.

Messenger: And if he wants to live among white people, or become part of them, he should have the freedom to do so?

Questioner: Not exactly, I don't....

Messenger: No, not exactly, but a little.

Questioner: Because I don't know about that. I'm not sure I know what that means. I believe that a Negro should have the right in this country to go anywhere that his intelligence, his capacity, and his wealth can take him. In the same way that a white man has the right to go anywhere.

Messenger: But you don't believe that he should have some part of the country wherein he could be independent.

Questioner: I believe that he should have whatever he can get legitimately in the same way that the white man can get it.

Messenger: But at the present time you think that it's all nice for him to just take and make himself a floating people here to go any place he want to but not on anything other than the privilege to stir around freely in the other man's house.

Questioner: I think that he should have the right to own land, to own factories, there are Negroes who own factories, there are Negroes, but there aren't many...

Messenger: How is he going to own land and factories, when he's not even given the right to even be a citizen of the country, or rather, only in words. Out here, how can he build factories and dispose, or seek a market for his product to be put on equal with you, when you are the absolute one that is keeping him in the place, or status that he's in. You put him in that, well now how...

Questioner: One of the things I always try to do is to avoid arguing with people in the Nation of Islam, because so much of what they say is very powerfully put and you have put me in a position of arguing about these things.

Messenger: No, I'm just asking questions, as you have asked me questions. I just wanted to ask you a few on the basis of how the thing looked to you, since your purpose is for some solution of the present condition of the Negroes in America.

Questioner: I began, I think by saying that the solution is a very difficult thing, and solutions are not my specialty. I have never written an article proposing a solution for anything.

Messenger: No sir.

Questioner: I don't write solutions, I write analysis, and I write to understand things. I'm not a.....

Messenger: I should have said to get to a better understanding, and then ask you, what have you done, what do you think?

Questioner: I think that I treat people as human beings irrespective of what their backgrounds and origins are. I would like everybody to treat everybody that way. There's a lot of evil in the world. Whether it comes because God wills it, or because God allows it. Whatever it is, I don't know, but there's a lot of evil in the world; I would like to see it removed. I am not the kind of person that can go out and remove it, I try to remove it from around me, as much as possible, and I try to teach the people of whom I am personally responsible to do likewise. I act as a human being towards other human beings. And I say I have confidence to a certain extent, this idea has been developing and spreading to a greater degree than use to be the case. I would like to see us move in that direction; this is the way I look at things. This may be naive, it may be optimistic, it may even be religious, I don't know.

Messenger: May I say this, that since you say that you know that there is a lot of evil in the world and you would like to see it removed, how are you going to remove evil if you're going to try and associate evil with good, you can't remove evil by associating it with...

Questioner: No, I disagree with you, I believe that good and evil must be associated, that's the way you change people.

Messenger: Well then you really don't want it removed.

Questioner: For example, no, suppose you take prison, take a man who commits a crime, I think a man who commits, the best way to avoid, to help a man who commits a crime, is to not put him with other criminals, but to put him among good people. Why do we put him among criminals? Because it's cheaper that way, it's like building a factory, so you take all the sick people and you put them in the hospital and we know very well that if a man is sick it's better for him not to be among sick people, but to be among healthy people, and in his own family, but we put them together with all sick people because they have x-ray machines, and big equipment, and so on. It's a matter not of knowing that this is the best way, but this is the cheapest way, and the cheapest way is not always the best way. So I don't believe, I believe that the way to eliminate evil, when a child does something wrong, and he does an evil thing, I don't mean that he's evil, but he does a thing that is evil, you don't immediately relegate him to all evil, you keep him among good people, to show him the proper way, and I believe that this is to the extent that this is possible, we aught to do it. So I believe that bringing the example of good to those who are evil.

Messenger: If you have a sick patient as you spoke upon, that which is a very good answer here, to what we are talking on, of good and evil. If you want to cure a person, if you are in a position, if you want to cure a person of a disease, could you cure that person of the disease without going at the root cause of disease?

Questioner: Well, let me say yes.

Messenger: How could you cure him?

Questioner: Well, you could not, you would have to get at the cause of his disease.

Messenger: You'll have to get the cause.

Questioner: Right.

Messenger: Alright. Then the only way you can cure evil, you have to get after the cause.

Questioner: Right.

Messenger: Yes sir. Well this means....

Questioner: I don't mean that, I don't believe that, that from that it follows you must separate evil from good. There is no such thing as pure evil, or pure good anyway, in my book. I think we all have, the best of us as the old phrase goes, have some evil in us, and the most evil of us have some good in us.

Messenger: We don't say that...

Questioner: I'm not saying that this is your view.

Messenger: No, we're speaking, I'm speaking mine, and you're speaking yours,

Questioner: Right

Messenger: Alright. Let us take a look at the thing. We certainly know that there is some good in everything, we certainly know that. And there is nothing that we have come across that is perfect in good. We have found some defect in good, and we have found so much good until that which we have discovered that we probably could consider a little defect, is not enough to affect the predominate percentage of good. So it is just the opposite in evil, here is something that's so filled with evil, that the little good in it can't affect the dominate.

Questioner: Those are the easy cases, Mr. Muhammad, those are the very easy cases, where it's 99% good and 1% evil, or it's 99% evil and 1% good. But human life unfortunately, at least the way I see it is made up of the difficult cases mostly, where it's hard to know what the balance is. You see. For example people, do you read what white people say about Negroes, many white people say they're all no good, look at what they do, the other day they threw a policeman off the roof in New York, or they did this, or they did that. So my answer is, well not all Negroes do believe these things. I have met many Negroes who are fine people, and I would prefer to associate with them, than to associate with many white people who I regard as evil. Then the white people you say, well all the white people are devils, they're all evil. Well I look around at many white people and I don't find them evil at all.

Messenger: You don't find them at all evil?

Questioner: No.

Messenger: You just a while ago have never found anything good, total good.

Questioner: Look at another thing, that whoever has produced the human being the way he is or what we have done, or human beings have done with what....

Messenger: Good human beings.

Questioner: Yes. I'm not speaking of the exploitation of one group over another, but I'm referring, that's, although I agree that's quite true, but I'm looking at something else, the mixture of good and evil, take such a thing for example as, if you'll excuse my mentioning such matters, the physical, sexual attraction between male and female. Physical and sexual attraction between male and female is centered around certain organs of the body, the male and female body.

Messenger: It's his nature, that's all.

Questioner: These organs, at the same time that they are the organs that attract the male and female to each other, are also the organs which produce the things which male and female or human beings detest at the same time. In other words, we have what is called a genitourinary system, the excretory and the genital system are the same organs, now that to me is a curious thing. And here is a mixture of what we regard as evil and what we regard as attractive and good, all joined together. The thing that produces the seed, which produces human beings, which must be, we must regard as a good, is also the organ that produces waste which we detest.

Messenger: Yes.

Questioner: Now there is a mixture, and this to me expresses human life.

Messenger: This is the way you look at it. Let me present my own personal observation and candid things about this in the root I get my ideal. If you try to eliminate the cause of evil, you have to go at the root of the evil cause.

Questioner: You have to be able to recognize it.

Messenger: You have to know it, and recognize it as true, and remove the cause as a man knows it. Here set in my flesh are certain diseases, that he can medicate maybe for many years, and never cure, but if he go after the root of that thing, he could cure it overnight. Just so it is with the people of today. All over the Earth there is dissatisfaction, and the dissatisfaction and disagreement is due to evil, and the only way to cure it now, since it's become universal or has universally spreaded and affects every human being, we have to go and diagnose the nation and find the cause. After diagnosing the nation, get rid of the cause. We can't say medicate it, because the prophets act as that medication, and they are turned down in what they were worth, so now go and get the root of that, dig up the root, and throw it out, and then you'll be rid of it.

Questioner: Well, on that level, I can certainly agree with what you're saying.

Messenger: Well that's exactly what I'm getting at; in fact, that's the work today. It's to get rid of the cause. So I have enjoyed talking with you.

Questioner: Well, thank you very, very much, I'm very grateful to you. I'm very honored to meet you and to talk with you about these things. I'm very grateful to you for taking all of this time. I really appreciate it; I know that you have many things to do.

Messenger: That's alright, we have maybe lots of getting around this Earth, and we must remember, that we don't know how many days that we will be getting around this Earth together. I don't know how many days it will be before we are separated and won't be getting around together; however, we do know this, that we are two people, that some of us will be getting around together for along time, and we have to come to some understanding.

Questioner: Long before we separate, we'll be together for quite awhile and I hope we can be together in peace. And I feel for one that the Negro, the darker have to much to contribute to the world for the white people to be able to afford this separation. In a sense, you might say that it's almost a kind of a selfish view point of my own, while I don't mean from the sense of exploiting what the Negro people, what they're talents are, but rather to adopt them in an interchange, and a fair interchange, and an equal interchange, and this is the kind of ideal that I would hold up. That may be a form of religion too.

Messenger: Well, that answer that you gave there is natural, that's the nature of you being a member of the people who have dominated us and still want's to do so. You don't want America's white brother of yours dominating you, you want to be as independent as he. I would not want to go to Africa and be dominated by my black brothers there; I would want a separate place here. And I'll rule myself as you are ruling yours, and especially here now since the spirit of self has become now dominate over the inferior spirit of depending upon others. It's so dominate to us today, we just can't agree with you or no other white people on being among you and

102

you the master, and we the slave, no. We are just like you, we want something for ourself. And if we have good ideas, and they were founded among the institution of learning that you have built or created, let us take them and go for ourself. We just don't feel that way, as a subject to other people.

Questioner: I don't think you want to.

Messenger: And especially when that people are so hostile that we want to live among them. So, they're so evil, that we even cannot even speak to them hardly in certain places, in the country without getting in something, or going away. We would have thought that we was never in the sight of such people. We are today like that; we're getting more like that. We even hate the day our father was put here on this part of the planet. We hate the day of the evil done to our people we see going on night and day. And we are more wide awake to an understanding and sensitive to the hurt than we were yesterday. We were not even sensitive to the hurt yesterday because we did not even have knowledge of the hurt. Now today we have the knowledge of the hurt, as a man have the knowledge of the hurt of a knife as soon as he see it pointed to his flesh, he know what it will do, and he wants to get away from it, so the same with us. We want to get away from it, we don't want no such hurting in or finding some way to get along and you stay a Negro and be my servant; no, no. No we don't want that regardless of the advancement in education; go and use it for ourself, and you can live wherever you want to; if you say this is your house, you live in your house. Let me go make a place for myself.

We have a big area on this planet Earth, that we can live in without living in America. Why is America so upset over us having a desire, even as much to go for ourself, when they have produced. They have produced our whole life, it's produced by them. Now if we have now been influenced, and another life is produced in us by another life or power that is in favor of us, or that is acting more gently towards us than you, why are you upset over our desire of getting away, when you say, "you are free to do so." If you said that a hundred years ago, of course you have made no provisions, for it was only word, and we are proving to you that, that was a mere word that you had spoken, and not anything sincere. You didn't have any institution for us going there for us. You just said we were free, but knowing that we couldn't exercise that particular freedom or right because you had not given it to us, you still held us under an invisible leash that we couldn't see at the time. But now we see the leash which shows that you have never helped us from under you or your power at all. I'm going to cut it, and then we know that we'll get rid of that leash.

Questioner: And then we feel terrible about it.

Messenger: Then you feel terrible about it; we want to know why you feel terrible, you should be happy. You should be happy; today you have claimed that we have never....

Questioner: Some of us are happy.

Messenger: But the main ones are not happy.

Questioner: No, the other ones are not happy.

Messenger: So, this is the thing I have before the world. I would like America to see her own position that she's taken, a position of trying to oppose the freedom of the Negro from going for himself, and while she preaches this doctrine at the same time, he's free. We're trying to do all we can to help you, how are you trying to help me to enjoy freedom for self, when you're trying to help me to stay and suffer the same thing that you have been given to me all my life, and now today you are asking me to continue on this. "I will do a little better than I have, I will let you sit over here, and let you sit in that chair." But that's still your chair. If I was sitting on the door step yesterday, that was your door step, and if you let me in the house today, that's still your house. I want to go and build a step for myself and a house for myself since I helped you build yours, and I've given that to you free and you did not respect me in doing that anymore than you did the animals that you used, and that you gave to me; to help a horse, a mule. I would like to do something for myself and you say you're to do right by me now," you're a citizen, as I am," but you're not practicing that with me. "And, I want to see all people free," but you're not practicing that even by your own people; that you want to see them free. You are turning one against the other all the time. And so that is not the thing we want now, we just want justice, as we are different people, as the whole entire world of life is built up like that, and created like that, and they all should be in the same sphere, each member to the

105

same, and not trying to hold this one. This is a foolish idea that America has, that she thinks that she can forever fool the Negro, and say, oh no, it's all right now, we understand, we still get to them.

She is secretly holding back the truth, "I don't want you Negroes to ever be independent for yourself, or have the freedom to do for yourself, I still want to be your boss. I will give you a little more on your salary, but still I want you as my worker." This don't make sense. We still will fight for the knowledge, and after all that we say, "Oh, this is my new job, to help him to do this", and he just adds another dollar, but that's not enough, only a share in his job. We don't share it, we're building up on the side here, a market, and we don't share in it. And when he fires us, we just have to sit down and open our mouths for whatever he drops in it and wait for him to hire us back. If we are trying to build up a factory like he has, then we won't be dependent upon him for employment. So this is the thing, America don't want us thinking of such, turning for self. They want to blind us and keep us thinking that everything I will think is for you, and not you think for yourself.

This is the open reaction: Telling a people that the way of understanding of the wise telling the slave, "I want you to continue to be my slave, and I will treat you better than I have, but my very nature as a master, I can't never make you part of the thing, because I brought you up settling for it, or rather settling as a slave. I brought you in for that purpose, and I can't now make you my equal. If I make you my equal, then I don't have my house, you probably will take it over, or you probably will go sit yourself in something that I'm already the boss of now, and I know it's mine and I can't do that, but I will give you an inferior station. I can't blind you and keep you thinking everything is alright" But somebody may listen clear enough after a while and see that they can't fool that child that sees through the sunlight. "It will say: naw, naw. It's day now I am getting out of this hell." That's why if any other one run off, he can cover him up. An atom that is wide awake, he jumps up and gets up. This is the thing, we want freedom for ourself, and we want to be a free people on this Earth and it's great, wide space, and build a future for our people as Israel, and Europe has done for their people.

They will invite you to Palestine with the backings of your brother to get there, and with the backings of your brother keeping you there. If you were removed, or the power of the backing of your brother removed, you probably couldn't stay, you see, why? Because the forces against you being there is too great for you to remain there, so it is now getting here, we could not go opposite America, unless we had enough power to force her and maintain ourselves after we get their, like you are. We cannot live here and teach, and have a future here as you could, and enjoy it long, because of the enemy's hatred and hostility against us. We won't have a country to aid us to escape from among the people who are enemies to us and who are always comfortable and ready to do the worse.

It was nice talking with you; I hope to read one of these books, and I do thank you for this one, and I am going to make a definite study of it and after I read the book, I will learn more about how you think of us.

Thank you for purchasing this book. We trust the reading was rewarding and enlightening.

We offer various titles and a comprehensive collection of Messenger Elijah Muhammad's works. These works include:

- **Standard Published Titles**
- **Unpublished & Diligently Transcribed Compilations**
- **Audio Cassettes**
- **Video Cassettes**
- **Audio CD's**
- **DVD's**
- **Rare Articles**
- **Year Books**
- **Annual Brochures**

You are welcomed to sample a listing of these items by simply requesting a FREE archive Catalog.

Our contact information is as follows:

Secretarius MEMPS Ministries
5025 North Central Avenue #415
Phoenix, Arizona 85012
Phone & Fax 602 466-7347
Email: cs@memps.com
Web: http://www.memps.com

Wholesale options are also available.

Made in the USA
Lexington, KY
29 November 2015